# Contents

# Introduction

*The unexamined life is not worth living—Socrates*

Socratic questioning is disciplined questioning that can be used to pursue thought in many directions and for many purposes, including: to explore complex ideas, to get to the truth of things, to open up issues and problems, to uncover assumptions, to analyze concepts, to distinguish what we know from what we don't know, and to follow out logical implications of thought. The key to distinguishing Socratic questioning from questioning per se is that Socratic questioning is *systematic, disciplined,* and *deep,* and usually focuses on foundational concepts, principles, theories, issues, or problems.

Teachers, students, or indeed anyone interested in probing thinking at a deep level can and should construct Socratic questions and engage in Socratic dialogue. When we use Socratic questioning in teaching, our purpose may be to probe student thinking, to determine the extent of their knowledge on a given topic, issue or subject, to model Socratic questioning for them, or to help them analyze a concept or line of reasoning. In the final analysis, we want students to learn the *discipline* of Socratic questioning, so that they begin to use it in reasoning through complex issues, in understanding and assessing the thinking of others, and in following-out the implications of what they, and others think.

In teaching, then, we can use Socratic questioning for at least two purposes:

1.  To deeply probe student thinking, to help students begin to distinguish what they know or understand from what they do not know or understand (and to help them develop intellectual humility in the process).

2.  To foster students' abilities to ask Socratic questions, to help students acquire the powerful tools of Socratic dialogue, so that they can use these tools in everyday life (in questioning themselves and others). To this end, we need to model the questioning strategies we want students to emulate and employ. Moreover, we need to directly teach students how to construct and ask deep questions. Beyond that, students need practice, practice, and more practice.

Socratic questioning teaches us the importance of questioning in learning (indeed Socrates himself thought that questioning was the only defensible form of teaching). It teaches us the difference between systematic and fragmented thinking. It teaches us to dig beneath the surface of our ideas. It teaches us the value of developing questioning minds in cultivating deep learning.

The art of Socratic questioning is intimately connected with critical thinking because the art of questioning is important to excellence of thought. What the word "Socratic" adds to the art of questioning is systematicity, depth, and an abiding interest in assessing the truth or plausibility of things.

Both critical thinking and Socratic questioning share a common end. Critical thinking provides the conceptual tools for understanding how the mind functions (in it's pursuit of meaning and truth); and Socratic questioning employs those tools in framing questions essential to the pursuit of meaning and truth.

The goal of critical thinking is to establish an additional level of thinking to our thinking, a powerful inner voice of reason, that monitors, assesses, and reconstitutes—in a more rational direction—our thinking, feeling, and action. Socratic discussion cultivates that inner voice through an explicit focus on self-directed, disciplined questioning.

In this guide, we focus on the mechanics of Socratic dialogue, on the conceptual tools that critical thinking brings to Socratic dialogue, and on the importance of questioning in cultivating the disciplined mind. Through a critical thinking perspective, we offer a substantive, explicit, and rich understanding of Socratic questioning.

To get you started in practicing Socratic questioning, we begin with the nuts and bolts of critical thinking (Part One), followed by some examples of Socratic dialogue (Part Two), and then the mechanics of Socratic dialogue (Part Three). The fourth and fifth sections focus on the importance of questioning in teaching, the contribution of Socrates, and the link between Socratic questioning and critical thinking.

### Socratic Questioning

- Raises basic issues
- Probes beneath the surface of things
- Pursues problematic areas of thought
- Helps students discover the structure of their own thought
- Helps students develop sensitivity to clarity, accuracy, relevance, and depth
- Helps students arrive at judgments through their own reasoning
- Helps students analyze thinking—its purposes, assumptions, questions, points of view, information, inferences, concepts, and implications

# Part One

## A Taxonomy of Socratic Questions
### Based in Critical Thinking Concepts

To formulate questions that probe thinking in a disciplined and productive way, we need to understand thinking—how it works and how it should be assessed. It is critical thinking that provides the tools for doing this, for analyzing and assessing reasoning. This is why understanding critical thinking is essential to effective Socratic dialogue.

As teachers, then, we need to understand the conceptual tools that critical thinking brings to Socratic questioning, and we need to foster student understanding of them. In this section we focus briefly on the following foundational critical thinking concepts:

1. **Analyzing thought** (focusing on the parts of thinking)
2. **Assessing thought** (focusing on standards for thinking)
3. **Analyzing questions by system** (distinguishing between questions of preference, fact and judgment)
4. **Developing prior questions** (focusing on questions we would need to answer before we could answer more complex questions)
5. **Identifying domains within complex questions** (focusing on questions we would need to answer within different subject areas or disciplines to adequately address a complex issue)

When we actively use these critical thinking concepts in the questions we formulate and ask, we raise thinking to higher levels of understanding and quality.

## Questions that Target the Parts of Thinking[1]

Using analytic questions in Socratic dialogue is foundational to understanding and probing reasoning. When we analyze, we break a whole into parts. We do this because problems in a "whole" are often a function of problems in one or more of its parts. Success in thinking depends on our ability to identify the components of thinking by asking questions focused on those components.

One powerful way to discipline questions, then, is to focus on the components of reasoning, or parts of thinking as illustrated by the following:

---

[1] For a deeper understanding of the structures of thought, see *A Miniature Guide to the Foundation of Analytic Thinking,* by Linda Elder, and Richard Paul, 2005, Foundation For Critical Thinking, www.criticalthinking.org. Also see *Critical Thinking: Tools for Taking Charge of Your Learning and Your Life,* by Richard Paul, and Linda Elder, 2006, Upper Saddle River, NJ: Pearson Prentice Hall.

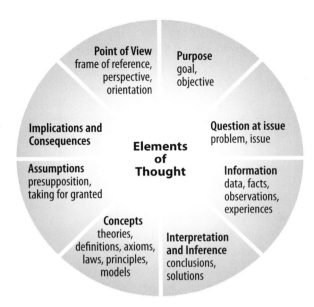

As you formulate questions, consider the following guidelines and sample questions:

1. **Questioning Goals and *Purposes*.** All thought reflects an agenda or purpose. Assume that you do not fully understand someone's thought (including your own) until you understand the agenda behind it. Some of the many questions that focus on purpose in thinking include:

   - What is your purpose right now?
   - What was your purpose when you made that comment?
   - Why are you writing this? Who is your audience? What do you want to persuade them of?
   - What is the purpose of this assignment?
   - What are we trying to accomplish here?
   - What is our central aim or task in this line of thought?
   - What is the purpose of this chapter, relationship, policy, law?
   - What is our central agenda? What other goals do we need to consider?

2. **Questioning *Questions*.** All thought is responsive to a question. Assume that you do not fully understand a thought until you understand the question that gives rise to it. Questions that focus on questions in thinking include:

   - I am not sure exactly what question you are raising. Could you explain it?
   - What are the main questions that guide the way you behave in this or that situation?

- Is this question the best one to focus on at this point, or is there a more pressing question we need to address?
- The question in my mind is this… Do you agree or do you see another question at issue?
- Should we put the question (problem, issue) this way… or that…?
- From a conservative viewpoint the question is…; from a liberal viewpoint it is… Which is the most insightful way to put it, from your perspective?
- What questions might we be failing to ask that we should be asking?

3. **Questioning *Information,* Data, and Experience.** All thoughts presuppose an information base. Assume that you do not fully understand the thought until you understand the background information (facts, data, experiences) that supports or informs it. Questions that focus on information in thinking include:
   - On what information are you basing that comment?
   - What experience convinced you of this? Could your experience be distorted?
   - How do we know this information is accurate? How could we verify it?
   - Have we failed to consider any information or data we need to consider?
   - What are these data based on? How were they developed? Is our conclusion based on hard facts or soft data?

4. **Questioning *Inferences* and Conclusions.** All thought requires the making of inferences, the drawing of conclusions, the creation of meaning. Assume that you do not fully understand a thought until you understand the inferences that have shaped it. Questions that focus on inferences in thinking include:
   - How did you reach that conclusion?
   - Could you explain your reasoning?
   - Is there an alternative plausible conclusion?
   - Given all the facts, what is the best possible conclusion?

5. **Questioning *Concepts* and Ideas.** All thought involves the application of concepts. Assume that you do not fully understand a thought until you understand the concepts that define and shape it. Questions that focus on concepts in thinking include:
   - What is the main idea you are using in your reasoning? Could you explain that idea?
   - Are we using the appropriate concept, or do we need to reconceptualize the problem?
   - Do we need more facts, or do we need to rethink how we are labeling the facts?
   - Is our question a legal, a theological, or an ethical one?

6. **Questioning *Assumptions.*** All thought rests upon assumptions. Assume that you do not fully understand a thought until you understand what it takes for granted. Questions that focus on assumptions in thinking include:
   - What exactly are you taking for granted here?

- Why are you assuming that? Shouldn't we rather assume that...?
- What assumptions underlie our point of view? What alternative assumptions might we make?

7. **Questioning *Implications* and Consequences.** All thought is headed in a direction. It not only begins somewhere (resting on assumptions), it is also goes somewhere (has implications and consequences). Assume that you do not fully understand a thought unless you know the most important implications and consequences that follow from it. Questions that focus on implications in thinking include:

- What are you implying when you say...?
- If we do this, what is likely to happen as a result?
- Are you implying that...?
- Have you considered the implications of this policy (or practice)?

8. **Questioning *Viewpoints* and Perspectives.** All thought takes place within a point of view or frame of reference. Assume that you do not fully understand a thought until you understand the point of view or frame of reference that places it on an intellectual map. Questions that focus on point of view in thinking include:

- From what point of view are you looking at this?
- Is there another point of view we should consider?
- Which of these possible viewpoints makes the most sense given the situation?

## Questions that Target The Quality of Reasoning

Universal intellectual standards are the standards by which thinking is judged by educated and reasonable persons. Yet, most people are unaware of these standards. These standards include, but are not limited to, clarity, precision, accuracy, relevance, depth, breadth, logical-ness, and fairness.

Skilled thinkers explicitly use intellectual standards on a daily basis. They recognize when others are failing to use them. They recognize when they are failing to use them. They routinely ask questions specifically targeting the intellectual standards.

Here are some guidelines for assessing thinking, along with some questions routinely asked by disciplined thinkers, questions that can be used in a Socratic dialogue.

1. **Questioning *Clarity*.** Recognize that thinking is always more or less *clear*. Assume that you do not fully understand a thought except to the extent you can elaborate, illustrate, and exemplify it. Questions that focus on clarity in thinking are:

- Could you elaborate on what you are saying?
- Could you give me an example or illustration of your point?
- I hear you saying "_____." Am I hearing you correctly, or have I misunderstood you?

2. **Questioning *Precision*.** Recognize that thinking is always more or less *precise*. Assume that you do not fully understand it except to the extent that you can specify it in detail.

Questions that focus on precision in thinking are:
- Could you give me more details about that?
- Could you be more specific?
- Could you specify your allegations more fully?

3. **Questioning *Accuracy.*** Recognize that thinking is always more or less *accurate.* Assume that you have not fully assessed it except to the extent that you have checked to determine whether it represents things as they really are. Questions that focus on accuracy in thinking are:
- How could we check that to see if it is true?
- How could we verify these alleged facts?
- Can we trust the accuracy of these data given the questionable source from which they come?

4. **Questioning *Relevance.*** Recognize that thinking is always capable of straying from the task, question, problem, or issue under consideration. Assume that you have not fully assessed thinking except to the extent that you have ensured that all considerations used in addressing it are genuinely *relevant* to it. Questions that focus on relevance in thinking are:
- I don't see how what you said bears on the question. Could you show me how it is relevant?
- Could you explain what you think the connection is between your question and the question we have focused on?

5. **Questioning *Depth.*** Recognize that thinking can either function at the surface of things or probe beneath that surface to deeper matters and issues. Assume that you have not fully assessed a line of thinking except to the extent that you have determined the *depth* required for the task at hand (and compared that with the depth that actually has been achieved). To figure out whether a question is deep, we need to determine whether it involves complexities that must be considered. Questions that focus on depth in thinking are:
- Is this question simple or complex? Is it easy or difficult to answer?
- What makes this a complex question?
- How are we dealing with the complexities inherent in the question?

6. **Questioning *Breadth.*** Recognize that thinking can be more or less broad-minded (or narrow-minded) and that *breadth* of thinking requires the thinker to think insightfully within more than one point of view or frame of reference. Assume that you have not fully assessed a line of thinking except to the extent that you have determined how much breadth of thinking is required (and how much has in fact been exercised). Questions that focus on breadth in thinking are:
- What points of view are relevant to this issue?

- What relevant points of view have I ignored thus far?
- Am I failing to consider this issue from an opposing perspective because I am not open to changing my view?
- Have I entered the opposing views in good faith, or only enough to find flaws in them?
- I have looked at the question from an economic viewpoint. What is my ethical responsibility?
- I have considered a liberal position on the issue. What would conservatives say?

## Questions That Help Us Assess Reasoning

| | |
|---|---|
| **Clarity** | Could you elaborate further?<br>Could you give me an example?<br>Could you illustrate what you mean? |
| **Accuracy** | How could we check on that?<br>How could we find out if that is true?<br>How could we verify or test that? |
| **Precision** | Could you be more specific?<br>Could you give me more details?<br>Could you be more exact? |
| **Relevance** | How does that relate to the problem?<br>How does that bear on the question?<br>How does that help us with the issue? |
| **Depth** | What factors make this a difficult problem?<br>What are some of the complexities of this question?<br>What are some of the difficulties we need to deal with? |
| **Breadth** | Do we need to look at this from another perspective?<br>Do we need to consider another point of view?<br>Do we need to look at this in other ways? |
| **Logic** | Does all this make sense together?<br>Does your first paragraph fit in with your last?<br>Does what you say follow from the evidence? |
| **Significance** | Is this the most important problem to consider?<br>Is this the central idea to focus on?<br>Which of these facts are most important? |
| **Fairness** | Do I have any vested interest in this issue?<br>Am I sympathetically representing the viewpoints of others? |

## The Art of Socratic Questioning Checklist

The following list can be used to foster disciplined questioning on the part of students. Students might take turns leading Socratic discussions in groups. During the process, some students might be asked to observe the students leading the discussion, and then afterwards provide feedback using the following guidelines (which all students should have a copy of during the discussion).

1. Did the questioner respond to all answers with a further question? _____

### Keeping Participants Focused on The Elements of Thought

1. Did the questioner make the *goal* of the discussion clear? _____
   (*What is the goal of this discussion? What are we trying to accomplish?*)

2. Did the questioner pursue relevant *information*? _____
   (*What information are you basing that comment on? What experience convinced you of this?*)

3. Did the questioner question *inferences,* interpretations, and conclusions where appropriate or significant? _____
   (*How did you reach that conclusion? Could you explain your reasoning? Is there another possible interpretation?*)

4. Did the questioner focus on key ideas or *concepts*? _____
   (*What is the main idea you are putting forth? Could you explain that idea?*)

5. Did the questioner note questionable *assumptions*? _____
   (*What exactly are you taking for granted here? Why are you assuming that?*)

6. Did the questioner question *implications* and consequences? _____
   (*What are you implying when you say…? Are you implying that…? If people accepted your conclusion, and then acted upon it, what implications might follow?*)

7. Did the questioner call attention to the *point of view* inherent in various answers? _____
   (*From what point of view are you looking at this? Is there another point of view we should consider?*)

8. Did the questioner keep the central *question* in focus? _____
   (*I am not sure exactly what question you are raising. Could you explain it? Remember that the question we are dealing with is…*)

9. Did the questioner call for a clarification of *context,* when necessary? _____
   (*Tell us more about the situation that has given rise to this problem. What was going on in this situation?*)

## Keeping Participants Focused on Systems For Thought

1. Did the questioner distinguish *subjective* questions from factual questions, from those requiring reasoned judgment within conflicting viewpoints? _____

    (*Is the question calling for a subjective or personal choice? If so, let's make that choice in terms of our personal preferences. Or, is there a way to come up with a single correct answer to this question? Or, are we dealing with a question that would be answered differently within different points of view? If the latter, what is the best answer to the question, all things considered?*)

2. Did the questioner keep the participants aware of alternative ways to think about the problem? _____

    (*Can you give me another way to think about this problem?*)

## Keeping Participants Focused on Standards For Thought

1. Did the questioner call for *clarification,* when necessary? _____

    (*Could you elaborate further on what you are saying? Could you give me an example or illustration of your point? Let me tell you what I understand you to be saying. Is my Interpretation correct?*)

2. Did the questioner call for more details or greater *precision,* when necessary? _____

    (*Could you give us more details about that? Could you specify your allegations more fully?*)

3. Did the questioner keep participants sensitive to the need to check facts and verify the *accuracy* of information? _____

    (*How could we check that to see if it is true? How could we verify these alleged facts?*)

4. Did the questioner keep participants aware of the need to stick to the question on the floor; to make sure their "answers" were *relevant* to the question being addressed at any given point? _____

    (*I don't see how what you said bears on the question. Could you explain what you think the connection is?*)

5. Did the questioner keep participants aware of the complexities in the question on the floor. Did the questioner ask participants to think deeply about *deep* issues? _____

    (*What makes this a complex question? How does your answer take into account the complexities in the question?*)

6. Did the questioner keep participants aware of multiple points of view when dealing with *broad* questions? _____

    (*We have looked at the question from an economic point of view. Now let's look at it from an ethical point of view. We have considered a liberal position on the issue, what would conservatives say? We have considered what you think about the situation, but what would your parents think?*)

### Keeping Participants Actively Engaged in the Discussion

1. Did the questioner think aloud along with the participants? _____

    (*I understand you to be saying.... I think this is a very complex question, and so I am not sure how to answer this. I would summarize the discussion thus far in the following way....*)

2. Did the questioner allow sufficient time for the participants to formulate their answers? _____

3. Did the questioner ensure that every contribution was sufficiently dealt with in some way? _____

4. Did the questioner periodically summarize where the discussion was in accomplishing its agenda? What questions had been and what questions had not yet been answered? _____

5. Did the discussion proceed smoothly with the various contributions being effectively blended into an intelligible whole? _____

## Four Directions in Which to Pursue Thought

There is another way to classify, and so arrange in our minds, questions we can ask to help stimulate student thought. This approach emphasizes four directions in which thought can be pursued and presupposes the elements of reasoning. As you examine the following diagram, you will see that all of the elements of reasoning are accentuated—except the question at issue and the conceptual dimension of thought. (See the diagram on the next page.)

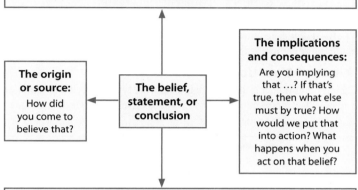

**Opposing thoughts and objections:**
How would you answer someone who said ...? What might these people say? How could someone else look at this? Why? Why do you think your way of looking at it is better?

**The origin or source:**
How did you come to believe that?

**The belief, statement, or conclusion**

**The implications and consequences:**
Are you implying that ...? If that's true, then what else must by true? How would we put that into action? What happens when you act on that belief?

**Support, reasons, evidence, and assumptions:**
How do you know? Are you assuming that ...? Is this a good assumption? What evidence do you have? Why is that relevant? How do you know your evidence is true? How are you conceiving of, thinking about the issue? Why?

This diagram, and the classifications implicit in it, helps accentuate the following important facts about thinking.

- All thinking has a history in the lives of particular persons.
- All thinking depends upon a substructure of reasons, evidence, and assumptions.
- All thinking leads us in some direction or other (has implications and consequences).
- All thinking stands in relation to other possible ways to think (there is never just one way to think about something).

This classificatory scheme highlights four ways we can help students come to terms with their thought:

- We can help students reflect on how they have come to think the way they do on a given subject. (In doing this, we are helping them examine the *history* of their thinking on that subject, helping them find the source or origin of their thinking.)
- We can help students reflect on how they support or might support their thinking. (In doing this, we are helping them express the reasons, evidence, and assumptions that underlie what they think.)

- We can help students reflect on what "follows from" their thinking, what implications and consequences their thinking generates. (In doing this, we are helping them recognize that all thinking entails or involves "effects" or "results" that we are obliged to consider.)
- We can help students reflect on how it is that people with points of view different from theirs might raise legitimate objections or propose alternative ways to think that they should take into account. (In doing this, we are helping them think more broadly, more comprehensively, more fair-mindedly.)

## Three Kinds of Questions

In approaching a question, it is useful to figure out what type it is. Is it a question with one definitive answer? Is it a question that calls for a subjective choice? Or does the question require us to consider competing answers.

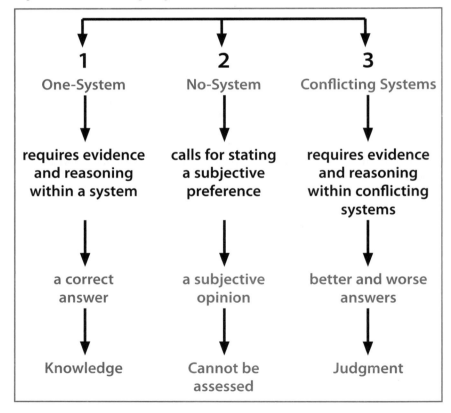

|  | **1** | **2** | **3** |
|---|---|---|---|
|  | **One-System** | **No-System** | **Conflicting Systems** |
|  | requires evidence and reasoning within a system | calls for stating a subjective preference | requires evidence and reasoning within conflicting systems |
|  | a correct answer | a subjective opinion | better and worse answers |
|  | Knowledge | Cannot be assessed | Judgment |

## Asking One-System, No-System, and Conflicting-System Questions

There are a number of ways to categorize questions for the purpose of analysis. One way is to focus on the type of reasoning required by the question. With one-system questions, there is an established procedure or method for finding the answer. With no-system questions, the question is properly answered in accordance with one's subjective preference; there is no "correct" answer. With conflicting-system questions, there are multiple competing viewpoints from which, and within which, one might reasonably pursue an answer to the question. There are better and worse answers, but no verifiable "correct" ones, since these are matters about which even experts disagree (hence the "conflict" from system to system).

To determine which of these three types of questions we are dealing with (in any given case) we can ask the following procedure: Are there relevant facts we need to consider in answering the question? If so, then either the facts alone settle the question (and we are dealing with a question of procedure), or the facts can be interpreted in different ways (and the question is debatable). If there are no facts we need to consider, then it is a matter of personal preference. Remember, if a matter is not one of personal preference, then there must be some facts that bear on the question. If the facts settle the question, then it is a "one-system" procedural question.

We want students to become comfortable with this schema of question types, to come to understand it in such a way that eventually they use it intuitively in their thinking. We want them to learn to ask and responsibly answer questions of reasoned judgment, to recognize when a question is complex, and to learn how to work their way through those complexities.

### Questions of Procedure (established- or one-system)

These include questions with an established procedure or method for finding the answer. These questions are settled by facts, by definition, or both. They are prominent in mathematics, as well as the physical and biological sciences. Examples:

- What is the boiling point of lead?
- What is the size of this room?
- What is the differential of this equation?
- How does the hard drive on a computer operate?
- What is the sum of 659 and 979?
- How is potato soup prepared, according to established Polish tradition?

### Questions of Preference (no-system)

Questions with as many answers as there are different human preferences (a category in which subjective taste rules). Examples:

- Which would you prefer, a vacation in the mountains or one at the seashore?
- How do you like to wear your hair?

- Do you like to go to the opera?
- What color scheme do you prefer in your house?

### Questions of Judgment (conflicting-systems)

Questions requiring reasoning, but with more than one arguable answer. These are questions that make sense to debate, questions with better-or-worse answers (well-supported and reasoned or poorly-supported and/or poorly-reasoned answers). Here we are seeking the best answer within a range of possibilities. We evaluate answers to such questions using universal intellectual standards such as breadth, depth, logicalness, and so forth. These questions are predominant in the human disciplines (history, philosophy, economics, sociology, art, and so on). Examples:

- How can we best address the most basic and significant economic problems of the nation today?
- What can be done to significantly reduce the number of people who become addicted to illegal drugs?
- How can we balance business interest and environmental preservation?
- Is abortion justifiable?
- How progressive should the tax system be?
- Should capital punishment be abolished?
- What is the best economic system for this particular country?

Many texts claim to foster critical thinking by teaching students to divide all statements into facts and opinions. When they do so, students fail to grasp the significance of dialogical thinking and reasoned judgment. When an issue is fundamentally a matter of fact (for example, "What is the weight of this block of wood?" or "What are the dimensions of this figure?"), there is no reason to argue about the answer; one should carry out the process that yields the correct answer. Sometimes this might require following complex procedures. In any case, weighing and measuring, the processes needed for the questions above, are not typically matters of debate.

On the other hand, questions that raise matters of mere opinion, such as "What sweater do you like better?" "What is your favorite color?" or "Where would you like to spend your vacation?", do not have a *correct* answer since they ask us merely to express our personal *preferences.*

However, most of the important issues we face in our lives are not exclusively matters of fact or matters of preference. Many require a new aspect: that we reason our way to conclusions while we take the reasoned perspectives of others into account. As teachers, we should be clear in encouraging students to distinguish these three different situations: the ones that call for facts alone, the ones that call for preference alone, and the ones that call for reasoned judgment. When, as members of a jury, we are called upon to come to a judgment of innocence or guilt, we do not settle questions of pure fact, and we are certainly not expected to express our subjective preferences.

Students certainly need to learn procedures for gathering facts, and they doubtless need to have opportunities to express their preferences, but their most important need is to *develop their capacities for reasoned judgment.* They need to know how to come to conclusions of their own based on evidence and reasoning of their own within the framework of their own perspectives—while also considering the perspectives of relevant others. Their values and preferences will, of course, play a role in their perspectives and reasoning, but their perspectives should not be a matter of pure opinion or sheer preference. We should not believe in things or people just because we *want* to. We should have good reasons for our beliefs, except, of course, where it makes sense to have pure preferences. It makes sense, if you so choose, to prefer butterscotch to chocolate pudding, but it does *not* make sense to prefer taking advantage of people rather than respecting their rights.

In a Socratic dialogue, we can help students distinguish among questions of fact, preference, and judgment. To help students do this, consider the following types of questions we might ask during a dialogue.

- What type of question are we addressing?
- Is this a question with one right answer?
- Is it a question asking for our preference? In other words, can we answer it by simply saying what we like or want?
- On the other hand, is it a question that calls on us to use reasoned judgment to come to a conclusion? In other words, is it a question that allows for more than one reasonable way to answer it? If so, and before we answer the question, what viewpoints are important to consider? Which viewpoints are more reasonable, given the evidence?

## Questioning Questions: Identifying Prior Questions

Whenever we are dealing with complex questions, one tool useful in disciplining our thinking is that of identifying questions presupposed in a question that is our direct concern. In other words, because questions often presuppose other questions having been answered, it is often useful to prepare to answer a question by figuring out what "prior" questions it assumes, or, alternatively, what other questions it would be helpful for us to answer first, before we try to answer the immediate question at issue. This is especially important when dealing with complex questions. In other words, it is useful to approach a complex question by first formulating and then answering simple questions embedded in the question, questions we must answer before trying to answer the larger, more complex question.

Hence, to answer the question "What is multiculturalism?" it would be helpful to first settle the question, "What is culture?" And to settle that question, it would be helpful to answer the question, "What are the factors about a person (nationality, religion, ideology, place of birth, and so forth) that determine what culture he or she belongs to?"

To construct a list of prior questions, begin by writing down the main question you are focused on. Then formulate as many questions as you can think of that you would have to answer, or it would be helpful to answer, before answering the first. Then take this list and determine what question or questions you would have to answer, or it would be helpful to answer, prior to answering these questions. Continue, following the same procedure for every new set of questions on your list.

As you proceed to construct your list, keep your attention focused on the first question on the list as well as on the last. If you do this, you should end up with a list of questions that shed light on the logic of the first question.

As an example of how to construct logically prior questions, consider this list of questions we would need to answer to address the larger question, "What is history?"

- What do historians write about?
- What is "the past?"
- Is it possible to include all of the past in a history book?
- How many of the events during a given time period are generally excluded in a history of that period?
- Is more information excluded than is included?
- How does a historian know what to emphasize?
- Do historians make value judgments in deciding what to include and what to leave out?
- What variables might influence a historian's viewpoint?
- Is it possible to simply list facts in a history book, or does all history writing involve interpretations as well as facts?
- Is it possible to decide what facts to include and exclude without adopting a historical point of view?
- How should we judge a historical interpretation?
- How should we judge a historical point of view?

## Asking Complex Interdisciplinary Questions

When addressing a complex question covering more than one domain of thought, make each domain explicit. Does the question, for example, include an economic dimension? Does it include a biological, sociological, cultural, political, ethical, psychological, religious, historical, or some other dimension? For each dimension of thinking inherent in the question, formulate questions that force you to consider complexities you otherwise may miss.

When focusing on domains within questions, consider such questions as:

- What are the domains of thinking inherent in this complex question?
- Am I dealing with all the relevant domains within the question?
- Are we leaving out some important domains?

The following figure shows some of the domains that might be embedded in a complex question:

Mathematics and
Quantitative Disciplines

Physical and Life
Sciences

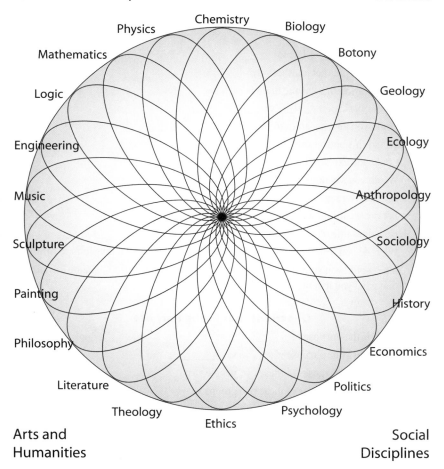

Arts and
Humanities

Social
Disciplines

This diagram was adapted from a diagram created by John Trapasso.

## Further Questions for Socratic Dialogue

### Questions of Clarification

- What do you mean by _____?
- What is your main point?
- How does _____ relate to _____?
- Could you put that another way?
- What do you think is the main issue here?
- Is your basic point _____ or _____?
- Could you give me an example?
- Would this be an example: _____?
- Could you explain that further?
- Would you say more about that?
- Why do you say that?
- Let me see if I understand you; do you mean _____ or _____?
- How does this relate to our discussion/problem/issue?
- What do you think John meant by his remark? What did you take John to mean?
- Jane, would you summarize in your own words what Richard has said? Richard, is that what you meant?

### Questions that Probe Purpose

- What is the purpose of _____?
- What was your purpose when you said _____?
- How do the purposes of these two people vary?
- How do the purposes of these two groups vary?
- What is the purpose of the main character in this story?
- How did the purpose of this character change during the story?
- Was this purpose justifiable?
- What is the purpose of addressing this question at this time?

## Questions that Probe Assumptions

- What are you assuming?
- What is Karen assuming?
- What could we assume instead?
- You seem to be assuming _____. Do I understand you correctly?
- All of your reasoning depends on the idea that _____. Why have you based your reasoning on _____ rather than _____?
- You seem to be assuming _____. How would you justify taking this for granted?
- Is it always the case? Why do you think the assumption holds here?

## Questions that Probe Information, Reasons, Evidence, and Causes

- What would be an example?
- How do you know?
- What are your reasons for saying that?
- Why did you say that?
- What other information do we need to know before we can address this question?
- Why do you think that is true?
- Could you explain your reasons to us?
- What led you to that belief?
- Is this good evidence for believing that?
- Do you have any evidence to support your assertion?
- Are those reasons adequate?
- How does that information apply to this case?
- Is there reason to doubt that evidence?
- What difference does that make?
- Who is in a position to know if that is the case?
- What would convince you otherwise?
- What would you say to someone who said _____?
- What accounts for _____?
- What do you think is the cause?
- How did this come about?
- By what reasoning did you come to that conclusion?
- How could we go about finding out whether that is true?
- Can someone else give evidence to support that response?

## Questions About Viewpoints or Perspectives

- You seem to be approaching this issue from _____ perspective. Why have you chosen this rather than that perspective?
- How would other groups/types of people respond? Why? What would influence them?
- How could you answer the objection that _____ would make?
- Can/did anyone see this another way?
- What would someone who disagrees say?
- What is an alternative?
- How are Ken's and Roxanne's ideas alike? Different?

## Questions that Probe Implications and Consequences

- What are you implying by that?
- When you say _____, are you implying _____?
- But if that happened, what else would also happen as a result? Why?
- What effect would that have?
- Would that necessarily happen or only probably happen?
- What is an alternative?
- If this and this are the case, then what else must be true?

## Questions About the Question

- How can we find out?
- Is this the same issue as _____?
- How could someone settle this question?
- Can we break this question down at all?
- Is the question clear? Do we understand it?
- How would _____ put the issue?
- Is this question easy or difficult to answer? Why?
- What does this question assume?
- Would _____ put the question differently?
- Why is this question important?
- Does this question ask us to evaluate something?
- Do we need facts to answer this?
- Do we all agree that this is the question?
- To answer this question, what other questions would we have to answer first?
- I'm not sure I understand how you are interpreting the main question at issue.

## Questions that Probe Concepts

- What is the main idea we are dealing with?
- Why/how is this idea important?
- Do these two ideas conflict? If so, how?
- What was the main idea guiding the thinking of the character in this story?
- How is this idea guiding our thinking as we try to reason through this issue? Is this idea causing us problems?
- What main theories do we need to consider in figuring out _____?
- Are you using this term "_____" in keeping with educated usage?
- What main distinctions should we draw in reasoning through this problem?
- What idea is this author using in her or his thinking? Is there a problem with it?

## Questions that Probe Inferences and Interpretations

- What conclusions are we coming to about _____?
- On what information are we basing this conclusion?
- Is there a more logical inference we might make in this situation?
- How are you interpreting her behavior? Is there another possible interpretation?
- What do you think of _____?
- How did you reach that conclusion?
- Given all the facts, what is the best possible conclusion?
- How shall we interpret these data?

# Part Two

## Socratic Questioning Transcripts

In this section, we provide four sample transcripts of Socratic dialogues. Each discussion focuses on helping students think critically about a concept or issue.

As you read through these transcripts, keep in mind the critical thinking concepts and tools we introduced in the previous section. Note the "intellectual moves" being made at each point in these dialogues—many of which we point out in parentheses.

Once you read through each of the transcripts—and we recommend that you read them aloud and dramatize them by your mode of reading—hopefully, you will then be motivated to read something of the history and theory of Socratic questioning in the next three sections. However, remember, the theory behind Socratic questioning is important only if it inspires you to learn how to question more systematically and deeply.

In short, Socratic questioning is a discussion:

1. led by a person who does nothing but ask questions,
2. that is systematic and disciplined (it is not a free-for-all),
3. wherein the leader directs the discussion by the questions he/she asks,
4. wherein everyone participating is helped to go beneath the surface of what is being discussed, to probe into the complexities of one or more fundamental ideas or questions.

As soon as you can, we suggest that you get some experience in leading a Socratic discussion. Follow these initial rules:

1. Pass out a transcript of one of the Socratic discussions in this section to your students. Dramatize the transcript by reading it aloud with your students. To do this, assign students to read the "student" parts of the transcript. You read the part of the teacher/questioner.
2. Make a list of questions that focus on a central idea you would like students to master (See pages 51–54 for sample lists).
3. Tell your students you want to try out what is called Socratic questioning and that you are just beginning, so you want them to help you in the process.
4. When leading a Socratic dialogue, tell your students that by the rules of Socratic questioning you are allowed only to ask questions. You are not allowed to answer any questions, except by asking another question.
5. Tell students that their job is to attempt to answer the questions you ask.
6. Think aloud as you lead the discussion. Don't rush. Base each of your questions on the answer given by the last student.
7. Take seriously every answer that is given. Make sure it is clarified so that everyone in class understands it.

8. Periodically, summarize what the class has figured out (by their answers). Also, indicate what you have not yet figured out.

Don't be surprised if your first attempts fall short of the mark. Be patient with yourself and your students. Skilled questioning requires patience and practice. Both you and your students must exercise patience. Both you and your students must practice.

# Transcript One

## Exploring the Mind and How it Works
### (Elementary School)

The following is a transcript of a 4th grade exploratory Socratic discussion. The discussion leader was with these particular students for the first time. The purpose was to determine how these children thought about a broad topic—the mind and how it works. The students were eager to respond and often seemed to articulate responses that reflected potential insights into the character of the human mind, the forces that shape us, the influence of parents and peer group, the nature of ethics, and of sociocentric bias. The insights are disjointed, of course, but the questions that elicited them and the responses that articulated them could be used as the basis for future discussions or assignments that deepen students' understanding of the mind and how it works.

While reading the transcript that follows, you may want to formulate questions that could have been asked but were not; student responses that could have been followed up, or other directions the discussion might have taken. Other ways to approach the manuscript would include explaining the function of each question or categorizing the questions.

*Teacher: How does your mind work? Where's your mind?*
Student: In your head. (Numerous students point to their heads)

*T: Does your mind do anything? (Exploring the Concept of "Mind")*
S: It helps you remember and think.
S: It helps, like, if you want to move your legs. It sends a message down to them.
S: This side of your mind controls this side of your body, and that side controls this other side.
S: When you touch a hot oven it tells you whether to cry or say ouch!

*T: Does it tell you when to be sad and when to be happy? How does your mind know when to be happy and when to be sad? (Questioning for Clarification and Probing Implications)*
S: When you're hurt it tells you to be sad.
S: If something is happening around you that makes you sad.
S: If there is lightning and you are scared.
S: If you get something you want.
S: It makes your body operate. It's like a machine that operates your body.

*T: Does it ever happen that two people are in the same circumstance, but one is happy and the other is sad? Even though they are in exactly the same circumstance? (Exploring Viewpoints or Perspectives)*
S: You get the same toy. One person might like it. The other gets the same toy and he doesn't like the toy.

T: *Why do you think that some people come to like some things and some
people seem to like different things?* *(Exploring Viewpoints or Perspectives)*
S: Cause everybody is not the same. Everybody has different minds and is built
different, made different.
S: They have different personalities?

T: *Where does personality come from?* *(Exploring the Concept of Personality)*
S: When you start doing stuff and you find that you like some stuff best.

T: *Are you born with a personality or do you develop it as you grow up?*
*(Probing the Cause)*
S: You develop it as you grow up.

T: *What makes you develop one rather than another?* *(Probing the Cause)*
S: Like, your parents or something.

T: *How can your parent's personality get into you?* *(Probing the Cause)*
S: Because you're always around them and then the way they act, if they think
they are good and they want you to act the same way, then they'll sort of
teach you and you'll do it.
S: Like, if you are in a tradition. They want you to carry on something that
their parents started.

T: *Does your mind come to think at all the way the children around you
think? Can you think of any examples where the way you think is like
the way children around you think? Do you think you behave like other
American kids?* *(Exploring Viewpoints and the Concept of Sociocentric
Thinking)*
S: Yes.

T: *What would make you behave more like kids around you than like Eskimo
kids?* *(Exploring Viewpoints or Perspectives)*
S: Because you're around them.
S: Like, Eskimo kids probably don't even know what the word "jump-rope" is.
American kids know what it is.

T: *And are there things that the Eskimo kids know that you don't know about?*
*(Exploring Viewpoints or Perspectives)*
S: Yes.
S: And also we don't have to dress like them or act like them, and they have to
know when a storm is coming so they won't get trapped outside.

T: *OK, so if I understand you then, parents have some influence on how you
behave and the kids around you have some influence on how you behave...*

*Do you have some influence on how you behave? Do you choose the kind of person you're going to be at all? (Probing Causes)*

S: Yes.

T: *How do you do that, do you think? (Probing Reasons and Causes)*

S: Well, if someone says to jump off a five-story building, you won't say OK. You wouldn't want to do that.

T: *Do you ever sit around and say, "Let's see, shall I be a smart person or a dumb one?" (Distinguishing Between the Concepts "Smart" and "Dumb")*

S: Yes.

T: *But how do you decide? (Probing Causes)*

S: Your grades.

T: *But I thought your teacher decided your grades. How do you decide? (Probing Causes)*

S: If you don't do your homework you get bad grades and become a dumb person. But if you study real hard, you'll get good grades.

T: *So you decide that, right? (Probing Causes)*

S: And if you like something at school, like computers, you work hard and you can get a good job when you grow up. But if you don't like anything at school, you don't work hard.

S: You can't just decide you want to be smart, you have to work for it.

S: You got to work to be smart just like you got to work to get your allowance.

T: *What about being good and being bad? Do you decide whether you're good or you're bad? How many people have decided to be bad? (Three students raise their hands) [to first student]: Why have you decided to be bad? (Distinguishing Between the Concepts of "Being Good" and "Being Bad")*

S: Well, I don't know. Sometimes I think I've been bad too long and I want to go to school and have a better reputation, but sometimes I feel like just making trouble and who cares.

T: *Let's see, is there a difference between who you are and your reputation? What's your reputation? That's a pretty big word. What's your reputation? (Exploring the Concept of Reputation)*

S: The way you act. If you had a bad reputation people wouldn't like to be around you and if you had a good reputation, people would like to be around you and be your friend.

T: *Well, but I'm not sure of the difference between who you are and who people think you are. Could you be a good person and people think you bad? Is that possible? (Clarifying Concepts and Probing Implications)*

S: Yeah, because you could try to be good. I mean, a lot of people think this one person's really smart, but this other person doesn't have nice clothes, but she tries really hard and people don't want to be around her.

T: *So sometimes people think somebody is real good and they're not, and sometimes people think that somebody is real bad and they're not. Like if you were a crook, would you let everyone know you're a crook? (Probing Interpretations and Implications)*

S [chorus]: NO!

T: *So some people are really good at hiding what they are really like. Some people might have a good reputation and be bad; some people might have a bad reputation and be good. (Questioning for Clarification)*

S: Like, everyone might think you were good, but you might be going on dope or something.

S: Does reputation mean that if you have a good reputation you want to keep it just like that? Do you always want to be good for the rest of your life?

T: *I'm not sure... (Clarification)*

S: So if you have a good reputation you try to be good all the time, don't mess up, and don't do nothing?

T: *Suppose somebody is trying to be good just to get a good reputation—why are they trying to be good? (Probing Reasons and Concepts)*

S: So they can get something they want and they don't want other people to have?

S: They might be shy and just want to be left alone.

S: You can't tell a book by how it's covered.

T: *Yes, some people are concerned more with their cover than their book. Now let me ask you another question. So, if it's true that we all have a mind and our mind helps us to figure out the world, and we are influenced by our parents and the people around us, and sometimes we choose to do good things and sometimes we choose to do bad things, sometimes people say things about us and so forth and so on...Let me ask you: Are there some bad people in this world? (Probing Implications)*

S: Yeah.

S: Terrorists and stuff.

S: Night-stalkers.

S: Hijackers.

S: Robbers.

S: Rapers.

S: Bums.

T: **Bums, are they bad?** *(Clarifying the Concept of "Bum")*

S: Well, sometimes.

S: The Ku Klux Klan.

S: The Bums…not really, cause they might not look good, but you can't judge them by how they look. They might be really nice and everything.

T: **OK, so they might have a bad reputation but be good, after you care to know them. There might be good bums and bad bums.** *(Questioning for Clarification and Probing Concepts)*

S: Iraqi guys and Machine Gun Kelly.

T: **Let me ask you, do the bad people think they're bad?** *(Exploring Perspectives)*

S: A lot of them don't think they're bad, but they are. They might be sick in the head.

T: **Yes, some people are sick in their heads.** *(Clarifying)*

S: A lot of them (bad guys) don't think they're bad.

T: **Why did you say Iraqi people?** *(Probing Reasons)*

S: Cause they have a lot o' terrorists and hate us and bomb us.

T: **If they hate us, do they think we are bad or good?** *(Probing Implications)*

S: They think we are bad.

T: **And we think they are bad? And who is right?** *(Exploring Perspectives)*

S: Usually both of them.

S: None of us are really bad!

S: Really, I don't know why our people and their people are fighting. Two wrongs don't make a right.

S: It's like if there was a line between two countries, and they were both against each other, if a person from the first country crosses over the line, they'd be considered the bad guy. And if a person from the second country crossed over the line, he'd be considered the bad guy.

T: **So it can depend on which country you're from who you consider right or wrong, is that right?** *(Exploring Perspectives)*

S: Like a robber might steal things to support his family. He's doing good to his family, but actually bad to another person.

T: **And in his mind, do you think he is doing something good or bad?** *(Exploring Perspectives and Implications)*

S: It depends what his mind is like. He might think he is doing good for his family, or he might think he is doing bad for the other person.

S: It's like the Underground Railroad a long time ago. Some people thought it was bad and some people thought it was good.

T: *But if lots of people think something is right and lots of people think something is wrong, how are you supposed to figure out the difference between right and wrong? (Probing Perspectives and Exploring the Concept of Ethics)*

S: Go by what you think!

T: *But how do you figure out what to think?*

S: Lots of people go by other people.

T: *But somebody has to decide for themselves, don't they?*

S: Use your mind?

T: *Yes, let's see, suppose I told you: "You are going to have a new classmate. Her name is Sally and she's bad." Now, you could either believe me, or what could you do? (Eliciting Reasonable Inferences)*

S: You could try to meet her and decide whether she was bad or good.

T: *Suppose she came and said to you: "I'm going to give you a toy so you'll like me." And she gave you things so you would like her, but she also beat up on some other people. Would you like her because she gave you things?*

S: No, because she said "I'll give you this so you'll like me." She wouldn't be very nice.

T: *So why should you like people? (Probing Reasons)*

S: Because they act nice to you.

T: *Only to you?*

S: To everybody!

S: I wouldn't care what they gave me. I'd see what they're like inside.

T: *But how do you find out what's on the inside of a person? (Seeking Information)*

S: You could ask, but I would try to judge myself.

## Commentary

The above discussion could have gone in a number of directions. For instance, rather than focusing on the mind's relationship to emotions, the teacher could have pursued the concept "mind" by asking for more examples of its functions, and having students analyze them. The teacher could have followed up the response of the student who asked, "Does reputation mean that if you have a good reputation you want to keep it just like that?" The teacher might, for instance, have asked the student why she asked that, and asked the other students what they thought of the idea. Such a discussion may have developed into a dialogical exchange about reputation, different degrees of goodness, or reasons for being bad. On the other hand, the concept "bad people" could have been pursued and clarified by asking students why the examples they gave were examples of "bad" people. Students may then have been able to suggest tentative generalizations, which could have been tested and probed through further questioning. Rather than exploring the influence of perspective on evaluation, the teacher might have probed the idea, expressed by one student, that no one is "really bad." The student could have been asked to explain the remark, and other students could have been asked for their responses to the idea. In these cases and others, the teacher has a choice between any number of equally thought provoking questions. No single question is the "right" question in a Socratic dialogue.

Realize, then, that Socratic questioning is flexible. The questions asked at any given point will depend on how students respond to the questions, what ideas the teacher wants to pursue, and what questions occur to the teacher during the discussion. Remember that Socratic questions generally raise basic issues, probe beneath the surface of things, and pursue problematic areas of thought.

# Transcript Two

## Helping Students Organize Their Thoughts for Writing
### (Middle School)

The following Socratic discussion represents an initial attempt to get students to think about what a persuasive essay is and how to go about preparing to write one. Of course, like all Socratic questioning dialogues, it goes beyond a single objective, for it also stimulates students to think critically in general about what they are doing and why. It helps them see that their own ideas, if developed, are important and can lead to insights.

T: *You are all going to be writing a persuasive essay, so let's talk about what you have to do to get your ideas organized. There are two ways to persuade people of something: by appealing to their reason, a rational appeal, and by appealing to their emotions, an emotional appeal. What is the difference between these? Let's take the rational appeal first. What do you do when you appeal to someone's reason? (Probing the Concept of Rational Appeal)*

S: You give them good reasons for accepting something. You tell them why they should do something or what they can get out of it or why it's good for them.

T: *But don't they already have reasons why they believe as they do? So why should they accept your reasons rather than theirs? (Probing Reasons)*

S: Well, maybe mine are better than theirs.

T: *But haven't you ever given someone, say your mother or father, good reasons for what you wanted to do, but they just did not accept your reasons even though your reasons seemed compelling to you? (Exploring Perspectives)*

S: Yeah, that happens a lot to me. They just say that I have to do what they say whether I like it or not because they are my parents.

T: *So is it hopeless to give people good reasons for changing their minds because people will never change their minds? (Exploring Implications)*

S: No, people sometimes do change their minds. Sometimes they haven't thought about things a lot or they haven't noticed something about what they're doing. So you tell them something they hadn't considered and then they change their minds...sometimes.

T: *That's right, sometimes people do change their minds after you give them a new way of looking at things or reasons they hadn't considered. What does that tell you about one thing you want to be sure to do in deciding how to defend your ideas and get people to consider them? What do you think, Tom?*

S: I guess you want to consider different ways to look at things, to find new reasons and things.

T: *Well, but where can you find different ways to look at things? What do you think, Janet? (Probing Different Perspectives, Probing Sources of Evidence)*

S: I would look in the library.

T: *But what would you look for, could you be more specific? (Questioning for Clarification and Precision)*

S: Sure. I'm going to write about why women should have the same rights as men, so I'll look for books on feminism and women.

T: *How will that help you find different ways to look at things? Could you spell that out further? (Questioning for Clarification)*

S: I think that certainly there will probably be different ideas in different books. Not all women think alike. Black women and white women and religious women and Hispanic women all have their own point of view. I would look for the best reasons that each give and try to put them into my paper.

T: *OK, but so far we have just talked about giving reasons to support your ideas, what I called in the beginning a rational appeal. What about the emotional side of things, of appealing to people's emotions? John, what are some emotions and why appeal to them? (Probing the Concept of Emotional Appeal)*

S: Emotions are things like fear and anger and jealousy, what happens when we feel strongly or are excited.

T: *Right, so do you know anyone who appeals to our emotions? Are your emotions ever appealed to? (Exploring Causes)*

S: Sure, we all try to get people involved in feeling as we do. When we talk to friends about kids we don't like we describe them so that our friends will get mad at them and feel like we do.

T: *How do we do this, could you give me an example, Judy? (Questioning for Clarification)*

S: OK, like I know this girl who's always trying to get her hands on boys, even if they already have girlfriends. So, I tell my friends how she acts. I give them all the details, how she touches them when she talks to them and acts like a dip. We really get mad at her.

T: *So what do you think, should you try to get your reader to share your feeling? Should you try to get their emotions involved? (Considering Possible Inferences)*

S: Sure, if you can.

**T: But isn't this the way propaganda works? How we get people emotional so that they go along with things they shouldn't? Didn't Hitler get people all emotional and stir up their hate? (Probing the Concept of Propaganda and Questioning for Clarification)**

S: Yeah, but we do that too when we play the national anthem, or when we get excited about Americans winning medals at the Olympics.

**T: So, what do you think of this Frank? Should we or shouldn't we try to get people's emotions stirred up? (Exploring Implications)**

S: If what we are trying to get people to do is good we should do it, but if what we are trying to get them to do is bad we shouldn't.

**T: Well, what do you think about Judy's getting her friends mad at a girl by telling them how she flirts with boys? (Clarifying Through Giving an Example)**

S1: Are you asking me?... I think she ought to clean up her own act first. (Laughter)

S2: What do you mean by that!

S1: Well, you're one of the biggest flirts around!

S2: I never flirt with boys who have girlfriends, and anyway, I'm just a friendly person.

S1: Yes, you are *very* friendly!

**T: OK, calm down you guys. There's an important point here. Sometimes we do act inconsistently and we criticize people for doing what we do. And that's one thing we should think about when writing our papers—are we willing to live by what we are preaching to others? Or another way to put this is by asking whether our point of view is realistic. If our point of view seems too idealistic then our reader may not be persuaded.**

**We don't have much time left today, so let me try to summarize. So far, we have agreed on a number of things important to persuasive writing: One, you need to give good reasons to support your point of view; two, you should be clear about what your reasons are; three, you should consider the issue from more than one point of view, including considering how your reader might look at it; four, you should check out books or articles on the subject to get different points of view; five, you should consider how you might reach your reader's feelings, how what you say ties into what they care about; six, following Judy's example, you should present specific examples and include the details that make your example realistic and moving; seven, in line with Frank's point,**

*you should watch out for contradictions and inconsistencies; and eight, you should make sure that what you are arguing for is realistic.*

*For next time, I would like you all to write out the introductory paragraph to your paper in which you basically tell the reader what you are going to try to persuade him or her of and how you are going to do it, that is, how the paper will be structured. When you come to class, you will be working in groups of threes to sharpen up what you have written.*

# Transcript Three
## Helping Students Think Deeply about Basic Ideas
### (High School)

In teaching, we tend to quickly skim past foundational ideas in order to get into ideas that are more derivative. This is part of the didactic viewpoint so prevalent in schooling at every level, the "school-is-giving-students-content-to-remember" perspective. What we need to do, in contrast, is stimulate student's thinking right from the beginning of the semester, especially about the most basic ideas in a subject. This will help motivate students, at the outset, to use their thinking in trying to understand things, so that they ground their thinking in foundational ideas that make sense to them. Then they build on those foundations.

**T: *This is a course in Biology. What kind of a subject is that? What do you know about Biology already? Kathleen, what do you know about it? (Clarifying the Concept of Biology)***

S: It's a science.

**T: *And what's a science? (Questioning for Clarification)***

S: Me? A science is very exact. They do experiments and measure things and test things.

**T: *Right, and what other sciences are there besides Biology? Marisa, could you name some?***

S: Sure, there's Chemistry and Physics.

**T: *What else?***

S: There's Botany and Math?

**T: *Math…math is a little different from the others, isn't it? How is math different from Biology, Chemistry, Physics, and Botany? Blake, what would you say? (Differentiating Between the Concept of Science and the Concept of Math)***

S: You don't do experiments in math.

**T: *And why not?***

S: I guess cause numbers are different.

**T: *Yes, studying numbers and other mathematical things is different from studying chemicals or laws in the physical world or living things and so forth. You might ask your math teacher about why numbers are different***

*or do some reading about that, but let's focus our attention here on what are called the life sciences. Why are Biology and Botany called life sciences? (Probing the Concept of "Life Science" and Connecting it to the Concepts of Biology and Botany)*

S: Because they both study living things.

T: *How are they different? How is Biology different from Botany? Jennifer, what do you think? (Distinguishing Between the Concept of Biology and the Concept of Botany)*

S: I don't know.

T: *Well, let's all of us look up the words in our dictionaries and see what is said about them.*

S: [Students look up the words]

T: *Jennifer, what did you find for Biology?*

S: It says, "The science that deals with the origin, history, physical characteristics, life processes, habits, etcetera…of plants and animals. It includes Botany and Zoology."

T: *So what do we know about the relationship of Botany to Biology? Rick? (Probing the Relationship Between Two Concepts)*

S: Botany is just a part of Biology.

T: *Right, and what can we tell about Biology from just looking at its etymology. What does it literally mean? If you break the word into two parts "bio" and "logy." Blake, what does it tell us? (Clarifying a Concept)*

S: The science of life or the study of life.

T: *So, do you see how etymology can help us develop insight into the meaning of a word? Do you see how the longer definition spells out the etymological meaning in greater detail? Well, why do you think experiments are so important to biologists and other scientists? Have humans always done experiments do you think? Marisa. (Probing Implications)*

S: I guess not, not before there was any science.

T: *Right, science didn't always exist. What did people do before science existed? How did they get their information? How did they form their beliefs? Peter. (Seeking Evidence and Exploring Perspectives)*

S: From religion.

T: *Yes, religion often shaped a lot of what people thought. Why don't we use religion today to decide, for example, what is true of the origin, history, and physical characteristics of life? (Exploring Perspectives)*

S: Some people still do. Some people believe that the Bible explains the origin of life and that the theory of evolution is wrong.

T: *What is the theory of evolution, Jose? (Exploring a Theory)*

S: I don't know.

T: *Well, why don't we all look up the name Darwin in our dictionaries and see if there is anything there about Darwinian theory.*

S: [Students look up the words]

T: *Jose, read aloud what you have found.*

S: It says "Darwin's theory of evolution holds that all species of plants and animals developed from earlier forms by hereditary transmission of slight variations in successive generations and that the forms which survive are those that are best adapted to the environment."

T: *What does that mean to you...in ordinary language? How would you explain that? Jose. (Questioning for Clarification)*

S: It means the stronger survive and the weaker die?

T: *Well, if that's true, why do you think the dinosaurs died out? I thought dinosaurs were very strong? (Questioning for Clarification and Probing Causes)*

S: They died because of the ice age, I think.

T: *So I guess it's not enough to be strong, you must also fit in with the changes in the environment. Perhaps fitness or adaptability is more important than strength. Well, in any case, why do you think that most people today look to science to provide answers to questions about the origin and nature of life rather than to the Bible or other religious teachings? (Probing Causes and Implications)*

S: Nowadays most people believe that science and religion deal with different things and that scientific questions cannot be answered by religion.

T: *And, by the same token, I suppose, we recognize that religious questions cannot be answered by science. In any case, how were scientists able to convince people to consider their way of finding answers to questions about the nature of life and life processes? Kathleen, you've been quiet for a while, what do you think?*

S: To me science can be proved. When scientists say something we can ask for proof and they can show us, and if we want we can try it out for ourselves.

T: *Could you explain that further? (Questioning for Clarification)*

S: Sure, in my chemistry class we did experiments in which we tested out some of the things that were said in our chemistry books. We could see for ourselves.

T: *That's right, science is based on the notion that when we claim things to be true about the world we should be able to test them to see if, objectively, they are true. Marisa, you have a comment?*

S: Yes, but don't we all test things. We test our parents and our friends. We try out ideas to see if they work.

T: *That's true. But is there any difference between the way you and I test our friends and the way a chemist might test a solution to see if it is acidic? (Questioning for Clarification, Probing Perspectives)*

S: Sure,…but I'm not sure how to explain it.

T: *Blake, what do you think?*

S: Scientists have laboratories; we don't.

T: *They also do precise measurements and use precise instruments, don't they? Why don't we do that with our friends, parents, and children? Adrian, do you have an idea why not? (Probing Perspectives and Implications)*

S: We don't need to measure our friends. We need to find out whether they really care about us.

T: *Yes, finding out about caring is a different matter than finding out about acids and bases, or even than finding out about animal behavior. You might say that there are two different kinds of realities in the world, the qualitative, and the quantitative, and that science is mostly concerned with the quantitative, while we are often concerned with the qualitative. Could you name some qualitative ideas that all of us are concerned with? Rick, what do you think? (Distinguishing Between the Concept of Qualitative Thinking and Quantitative Thinking)*

S: I don't know what you mean.

T: *Well, the word qualitative is connected to the word quality. If I were to ask you to describe your own qualities in comparison to your brother or sister, would you know the sort of thing I was asking you? (Clarifying the Concept of Qualitative Thinking)*

S: I guess so.

T: *Could you, for example, take your father and describe to us some of his best and some of his worst qualities as you see them? (Questioning for Clarification)*

S: I guess so.

T: *OK, why don't you do it? What do you think some of your father's best qualities are? (Questioning for Clarification)*

S: To me he is generous. He likes to help people out when they are in trouble.

**T:** *And what science studies generosity? (Questioning for Clarification)*

S: I don't know. None, I guess.

**T:** *That's right, generosity is a human quality. It can't be measured scientifically. There is no such thing as generosity units. So science is not the only way we can find things out. We can also experience qualities in the world. We can experience kindness, generosity, fear, love, hate, jealousy, self-satisfaction, friendship, and many, many other things as well. In this class, we are concerned mainly with what we can find out about life quantitatively or scientifically.*

*For next time, I want you to read the first chapter in your textbook and write a brief summary of the chapter's main points. When you come to class, I will divide you up into groups of four and each group together will write a short summary of the first chapter (without looking at the chapter, of course, but your notes can be used), and then we will have a spokesperson from each group explain your summary to the class. After that, we will have a discussion of the ideas mentioned. Don't forget today's discussion, because I'll be asking you some questions that will determine whether you can relate what we talked about today with what was said in your first chapter. Any questions? OK. See you next time.*

# Transcript Four

## Helping Students Think Seriously about
## Complex Social Issues
### (High School)

In the following discussion, Rodger Halstad, Homested High School Social Studies teacher, Socratically questions students about their views on the Middle East. He links up the issue with the holocaust during WWII and, ultimately, with the problem of how to correct one injustice without committing another.

T: *I thought what we'd do now is to talk a little about the Middle East. Remember we saw a film, "Let My People Go," which depicted some of the things that happened in the death-camps of Nazi Germany during World War II. Remember that? It's pretty hard to forget. Who do you hold responsible for what happened to the Jewish people during the holocaust, the Nazi holocaust of the 1940s and the late 1930s? Who do you hold responsible for that? (Seeking Logical Conclusions)*

S: Everyone. Um…

T: *What do you mean, "everyone?" (Questioning for Clarification)*

S: It started in Germany. My first thought goes to Hitler; then it goes to the German people that allowed him to take control without seeing what he was doing before it was too late.

T: *Would you punish all Germans? No? OK, then who would you punish?*

S: Hitler.

T: *OK. I think probably we'd all agree to that. Anyone else?*

S: Probably his five top men. I…I'm not sure…there are a lot of Nazis out there.

T: *Well, are you sure everyone was a member of the Nazi party? (Questioning Assumptions)*

S: Well, not all Germans were…um…

T: *Do you want to think about it?*

S: Yeah.

T: *How about somebody else? First of all, we all agree that somebody should have been punished, right? All right, these are not acts that should have gone unpunished. (Questioning for Clarification)*

S: Well, it'd be kind of hard, but, like, I think that every soldier or whatever, whoever took a life, theirs should be taken.

**T: *Every Nazi soldier who was in the camps? (Questioning for Clarification)***
S: Everyone who had something to do with what happened.

**T: *Everyone who had something to do with the killing of the people in the camps. The Jews, the gypsies, the opponents of Hitler, all those people. All the millions killed. Anybody that played a direct role. You would punish them. What if we had a corporal here, and the corporal said, "I only did this because I was ordered to do it. And if I didn't do it, my family was going to be injured, or something bad was going to happen to my family." Are you going to punish that corporal? (Exploring Ethical Implications)***
S: Well, I guess…well, I mean they still took a life, you know, but they were just following the rules. But I mean, you know, if you take a life…

**T: *What if they didn't take a life? What if they just tortured somebody?***
S: Then they, they should be tortured in the same way.

**T: *So you say anybody who was directly responsible for any injury, torture, murder, whatever in the camps; they themselves should get a similar kind of punishment. What about the people who were in the bureaucracy of the German government who set up the trains and the time schedule of the trains? What about the engineer on the train?***
S: Well, yeah, I guess…

**T: *All those people?***
S: Yeah, because if you think about it, if they hadn't of done that, they couldn't have gotten the people there.

**T: *OK, and what about the people standing on the streets while the Jews got in the trucks?***
S: No, I think that's going a little too far.

**T: *OK, so anybody who participates in any way in the arrest, the carrying out of all these activities, including even people who, ah…what about people who typed up the memos?***
S: Yeah, I guess

**T: *No, says Manual. Why no?***
S: Like, for example, if they're put under a lot of pressure. Like, ah, we're going to kill your family, we're going to hurt your family, put them in a concentration camp too.

**T: *Yes. Yes?***
S: It, it's just total…you just can't hold them responsible because their family… it's just like, ah…the next, the closest thing to them, and you can't just say you have to punish them because I don't think they did it on purpose. They

didn't do it because they wanted to see them suffer. They did it because they didn't want to see their family suffer.

T: *So you're saying that anyone who enjoyed what they were doing needs to be punished, right? What if I do it, but I don't enjoy it? (Questioning for Clarification)*

S: I don't think they should be punished.

T: *OK, suppose we brought all those people in here and asked them if they did it because they wanted to and they all said no. They all did it because they were ordered to. What then? How do we know if they enjoyed it or not?*

S: That's a good question.

S: Yeah.

S: Well, ah…that's why I think that it should maybe just be the leadership because they're the ones who made up the concentration camps, and they're the ones who tell the people to do it. And some people will want to do these things, and some people won't, and you can't determine who wants to do it and who doesn't.

T: *OK, suppose I'm Hitler and you are one of my top men and I order you to kill someone or you will be killed and you do it even if you didn't want to. Should you be punished? (Questioning for Clarification and Exploring Ethical Responsibility)*

S: Yeah, because you shouldn't be a Nazi in the first place.

T: *So any body who is in the camp who does these deeds—even though they did not want to—they should also be held responsible and punished? (Questioning for Clarification)*

S: You can't. There are too many of them. It's stooping to the Nazi's level by killing, by punishing all these people.

T: *So will you let some of them go free because you can't punish all of them? (Probing Implications)*

S: Right, you can't, you can't punish a whole entire group of people, that's like millions of people.

T: *Why can't you do that? (Probing Reasons and Implications)*

S: Because it's doing what they were doing to the Jewish people.

T: *Will we get some disagreement here, Jeannette?*

S: If you can't call a person responsible for making a decision, where does that leave society?

T: *What kind of decision? (Question for Clarification)*

S: They made a decision to follow the order.

**T:** *But what if they did it under duress? (Exploring Reasons)*

**S:** They could've…faced the responsibilities, you have to face responsibilities either way, you can't just do something.

**T:** *Suppose…suppose I say to you, "Jeanette, I want you to pull Bill's eyeballs out of his head. (Laughter) And if you don't do that, I am going to kill you, Jeanette." (Exploring Implications)*

**S:** I am responsible

**T:** *Are you responsible? (Questioning for Clarification)*

**S:** I'm responsible.

**T:** *You're going to die!*

**S:** I'm responsible!

**T:** *So we should punish you because you do this deed even though you would have died if you hadn't done it? (Questioning for Clarification and Probing Implications)*

**S:** No! It's still my decision.

**S:** But they, what if they were drafted into being in the Nazi camps and they were forced to do that—and they did not want to do that?

**S:** How did they force…

**S:** Just like we had American troops in Viet Nam, they were killing people.

**S:** And they were drafted.

**S:** A lot of people ran though.

**T:** *Time out! Time out, we have a real important discussion and that is the issue of the people who did not willingly do it, who did it because of an order. Are they, or are they not, responsible? (Probing Ethical Responsibility)*

**S:** I agree with Jeanette. They are responsible, they made the decision to do it—they have a choice, but some people I'm sure made the choice to die rather than to do this. I'm sure there were people that did that. And that was their decision because they could not go through with the order. You can't live with that. They went through it and made that decision. They have to live with what they did and they have to be punished for it because they took the lives of other people.

**T:** *Wait a minute. Do you know the story of Patty Hearst at all? I know it's ancient history to you. When she was kidnapped by a group called the SLA, she was brainwashed and she was beaten. She was abused and eventually she joins the group and they rob a bank and she had a part in the bank robbery. After she was freed, she was put on trial, and she argued that during the bank robbery, they had a gun on her and she didn't have any choice. Is she responsible for her acts in that bank robbery? Does she go* *free or do you punish her for the bank robbery?* *(Probing Reasons and Implications)*

S: That's a hard question. (Yeah, no fair) Was it proven that there was a gun on her?

T: *Yes, they had videotape. It was not clear whether there were bullets in the gun or so forth. There is tape of a gun.*

S: Well, if there's proof, that's different.

T: *What do you mean, "that's different?" (Questioning for Clarification)*

S: Well, different than someone who was a Nazi.

T: *No, no, let's not get to Nazis yet. Imagine you're on a jury, are you going to vote guilty or innocent? (Seeking Logical Inferences)*

S: Innocent.

T: *Why? (Probing Reasons)*

S: Because there was proof that she was forced; it wasn't a threat that something was going to happen. She was forced.

T: *Did she do it under threat of her own life? (Questioning for Clarification and Probing Reasons)*

S: Yes.

T: *All right. Suppose you, Leslie, are a Nazi, and you, Gayle, are neutral. Leslie tells Gayle, If you don't kill Ariel the Jew, you will be punished. Gayle kills Ariel the Jew. She does it because Leslie threatened her to do it. Is Gayle guilty? (Probing Reasons and Implications)*

S: No, I guess.

T: *But look. Do you see the inconsistency with the previous position? On the one hand, you say that Patty Hearst was not guilty, because she was forced, but on the other hand, you say that a Nazi is guilty even if they were forced, too? (Questioning for Clarification and Reasons, Pointing Out Contradictions)*

S: I think it's conditional.

T: *What is conditional? (Questioning for Clarification)*

S: Well, that, that the people are ultimately responsible for their actions because in the Patty Hearst case, she umm, it was a bank robbery, and that wasn't directly, I mean that was—are not supposed to steal people's money and that would affect people, but it's not physically, its not physical pain and it's not, you know, killing them, and so I think they should of um punish all the people who are in the Nazi camp because they were responsible for—physical pain and ah their deaths.

## Conclusion

Now that you have read through these transcripts, review Part One again perhaps focusing specifically on "Further Questions for Socratic Dialogue" (pp. 20–23). Then practice leading Socratic dialogues with your students. Before doing so, prethink the main question or issue you will be dealing with. What key ideas do you want to focus on? What conflicts might you expect in the dialogue? What is your main purpose?

Don't be overly concerned with your skill level as you work your way, with your students, through these discussions. Leading Socratic dialogues is an art, not a science. There may be any number of fruitful directions in which you might go at any moment in the discussion. Choose one direction and go there. If any given direction doesn't bear fruit, choose another. With practice, your skills will improve. Once you have had some practice in leading Socratic discussions, read through the rest of this guide to deepen your understanding of the importance of Socratic questioning in instruction, to learn how and when Socratic dialogue might be used, and to better understand the link between critical thinking and Socratic questioning.

# Part Three

## The Mechanics of Socratic Questioning

### Three Kinds of Socratic Discussion

We can loosely categorize three general forms of Socratic questioning and distinguish three basic kinds of preparation for each: spontaneous, exploratory, and focused. Each of these forms of questioning can be used to probe student thinking at any level of instruction—from elementary throughout graduate school.

All three types of Socratic discussion require developing the art of questioning. They require the teacher to learn a wide variety of intellectual moves and to develop judgment in determining when to ask which kinds of questions (realizing that there is rarely one best question at any particular time).

#### Spontaneous or Unplanned

When your teaching is imbued with the Socratic spirit, when you maintain your curiosity and sense of wonderment, there will be many occasions in which you will spontaneously ask students questions that probe their thinking. There will be many opportunities to question what they mean and explore with them how you might find out if something is true, logical, or reasonable. If one student says that a given angle will be the same as another angle in a geometrical figure, you may spontaneously question how the class might go about proving or disproving this assertion. If a student says, "Americans love freedom," you may spontaneously wonder aloud about what such a statement might mean (Does that mean, for example, that we love freedom more than other people do? Does it mean that we live in a free country? What would it mean to live in a free country? How would we know if we did? Does "freedom" mean the same thing to all Americans?). If in a science class a student says that most space is empty, you may spontaneously ask a question as to what that might mean and how you together might find out.

Such spontaneous discussions provide models of listening critically as well as exploring the beliefs expressed. If something said seems questionable, misleading, or false, Socratic questioning provides a way of helping students become self-correcting, rather than relying on correction by the teacher. Spontaneous Socratic discussion can prove especially useful when students become interested in a topic, when they raise an important issue, when they are on the brink of grasping or integrating a new insight, when discussion becomes bogged down or confused or hostile. Socratic questioning provides specific moves which can fruitfully take advantage of student interest. It can help you effectively approach an important issue. It can aid in integrating and explanding an insight, move a troubled discussion forward, clarify or sort through what appears confusing, and diffuse frustration or anger.

Although by definition there can be no preplanning for a particular spontaneous discussion, you can prepare yourself by becoming familiar and comfortable with generic Socratic questions, by developing the art of raising probing follow-up questions and by giving encouraging and helpful responses. Consider the following "moves" you might be prepared to make:

## Spontaneous Socratic Questioning "Moves"

- Ask for an example of a point a student has made, or of a point you have made.
- Ask for evidence or reasons for a position.
- Propose a counter-example or two.
- Ask the group whether they agree. (Does everyone agree with this point? Is there anyone who does not agree?)
- Suggest parallel or similar examples.
- Provide an analogy that illuminates a particular position.
- Ask for a paraphrase of an opposing view.
- Rephrase student responses clearly and accurately.

In short, when you begin to wonder more and more about meaning and truth, and so think aloud in front of your students by means of questions, Socratic exchanges will occur at many unplanned moments in your instruction. However, in addition to these unplanned wonderings, we can also design or plan out at least two distinct kinds of Socratic discussion: one that explores a wide range of issues and one that focuses on one particular issue.

## Exploratory

What we call exploratory Socratic questioning is appropriate when teachers want to find out what students know or think and to probe student thinking on a variety of issues. For example, you might use it to assess student thinking on a subject at the beginning of a semester or unit. You could use it to explore student values, or to uncover problematic areas or potential biases. You could use it to identify where your students are the most clear or the most fuzzy in their thinking. You can use it to discover areas or issues of interest or controversy, or to find out where and how students have integrated academic material into their thinking (and into their behavior). Such discussions can be used in introducing a subject, in preparing students for later analysis of a topic, or in reviewing important ideas before students take a test. You can use it to determine what students have learned from their study of a unit or topic, or as a guide to future assignments.

After an exploratory dialogue, you might have students take an issue raised in discussion and develop in writing their own views on the issue. Or you might have students form groups to further discuss the issue or topic.

With this type of Socratic questioning, we raise and explore a broad range of interrelated issues and concepts, not just one. It requires minimal preplanning or prethinking. It has a relatively loose order or structure. You can prepare by having some general questions ready to raise when appropriate by considering the topic or issue, related issues, and key concepts. You can also prepare by predicting students' likeliest responses and preparing some follow-up questions. Remember, however, that once students' thought is stimulated there is no predicting exactly where the discussion might go.

## Exploring Important Concepts

Teachers can use the following types of questions, in exploratory discussions, to foster students' conceptual abilities, and to help students begin to take ideas seriously. These are just a few of many possible examples:

- What are friends? Why do people have friends? Does having a friend ever cause problems? Is it hard to be a good friend? What is the difference between friends and best friends?
- What is the difference between wanting something and needing it?
- What is good? What is bad? What is the difference between good and bad?
- What are rules? What are they for? What is the difference between good rules and bad rules?
- What are the differences between people and animals?

## Focused

Much of the time you will approach your instruction with specific topics and issues to cover. In doing so, you might use focused Socratic questioning. To probe an issue or concept in depth, to have students clarify, sort, analyze and evaluate thoughts and perspectives, distinguish the known from the unknown, synthesize relevant factors and knowledge, students can engage in an extended and focused discussion. This type of discussion offers students the chance to pursue perspectives from their most basic assumptions through their furthest implications and consequences. These discussions give students experience in engaging in an extended, ordered, and integrated dialogue in which they discover, develop, and share ideas and insights. It requires preplanning or thinking through possible perspectives on an issue, grounds for conclusions, problematic concepts, implications, and consequences. You can further prepare by reflecting on those subjects relevant to the issue: their methods, standards, basic distinctions and concepts, and interrelationships—points of overlap or possible conflict. In preparing follow-up questions, you should consider, in advance, the likeliest student answers to original questions.

Consider the following examples of focused Socratic discussions, some of which would be used at the elementary level, others in the upper grades and beyond. Note that focused Socratic dialogue questions should be worked out in advance, but that the teacher should maintain flexibility to move among and beyond these questions depending on the answer a given question elicits. Again, remember that Socratic questioning is not a science. Any given Socratic discussion might take many directions.

## Thinking Through the Concept of Cooperation

If you are focused on the concept of cooperation, you want students to grasp, among other things, the fact that to understand any concept well is to understand its opposite well. To understand when we should not cooperate is as important as understanding when we should cooperate, if we are to understand "cooperation" at a deep level. Yet, too often, students are simply told to cooperate, as if cooperation were always desirable. Through a Socratic dialogue, we can help students begin to think critically about this concept.

The list of questions you construct for the Socratic dialogue might look something like this:

- What does it mean to cooperate?
- Can you think of a time when you cooperated? Explain.
- Can any one think of a time when you did not cooperate?
- Should you cooperate with your parents? If so, why?
- Should you cooperate with your teachers? If so, why?
- Should you cooperate with your friends? If so, why?
- Should you always cooperate?
- When should you?
- When should you not?
- When people want you to go along with something that you think is wrong, should you cooperate? What if people call you names if you refuse to cooperate, should you cooperate then?
- What would the world be like if no one ever cooperated with each other?
- What would it be like if everyone always cooperated?
- Are any problems created when people cooperate with one another?

## Thinking Through the Concept of Democracy

- What is a democracy?
- What does it mean to live in a democratic country?
- Can a democracy work well if people within it are uneducated? Why/why not?
- Can it work if people are not willing to find out about laws before voting on them? Why/why not?
- Is everything in a family decided democratically? Is anything? What about at school?
- What would it be like if everything were decided democratically?
- What would it be like if everything were decided democratically at home?
- What would it be like if everything were decided democratically at school?
- What would it be like if nothing were decided democratically?
- What is the difference between a democracy and a plutocracy?
- What is the difference between a democracy and an oligarchy?
- To what extent can a democracy thrive if people who are wealthy within the country have more power than people who are not wealthy?
- To what extent do we have democracy in this country? To what extent, a plutocracy?
- To what extent do wealthy people have more power in this country than people who lack wealth? Can you think of any examples?

## Thinking Through the Concept of Language

- What is language?
- What is the purpose of language?
- What are words?
- Can we use our words to hurt people? To help people?
- What would it be like if we didn't have words?
- Would life have meaning without words?
- How does the language we use influence the way we think?
- How does it influence our actions?
- Do people ever use language to manipulate other people?
- For example, if I tell you that I am your friend in order to get you to give me something of yours that I want, would this be an example of misusing language in order to manipulate you?
- Do people have a right to use language in any way they want?

## Thinking Through the Concept of a Friend

- What does it mean to be a friend?
- How do you know when someone is your friend?
- Can someone be nice to you and not be your friend?
- Can someone tell you things you might not want to hear and still be your friend?
- Is it possible for someone to not play with you and still be your friend?
- What is the difference between a friend and a classmate?
- Can your parent be your friend?
- Is it important to have friends?
- If someone is not your friend, how should you treat her/him?
- Is it possible to be friendless?
- How would you feel if you were friendless?
- Have you ever refused to be someone's friend when s/he wanted you to be?
- What is the difference between a friend and an enemy?
- Is it possible for someone to try to injure you and still be your friend?

## Thinking Through the Concept of Science

You might focus on a key concept within the subject you teach, such as science. Here are some questions you might ask to help students begin to think critically about science:

- What are the kinds of things that scientists do?
- Why is science important?
- What are some of the most basic assumptions scientists ask?
- What have we figured out using science?
- What are some things we should be able to figure out using science?
- How is science different from other fields of study?
- What are some of the branches of science?
- How would our lives be different if we didn't have science, or if no one thought scientifically?
- What are some of the limitations of science?
- Can science solve all our problems?
- Has science ever caused problems?

## Wondering Aloud About Truth and Meaning

Socratic discussion, guided by the teacher, in which students' thought is elicited and probed, allows students to develop and evaluate their thinking by making it explicit. By encouraging students to slow their thinking down and elaborate on it, Socratic discussion gives students the opportunity to develop and test their ideas—the beliefs they have spontaneously formed and those they learn in school. Through this process, students can synthesize their beliefs into a more coherent and better-developed perspective.

Socratic questioning requires teachers to take seriously what students say and think: what they mean, its significance to them, its relationship to other beliefs, how it can be tested, to what extent and in what way it is true or makes sense. Socratic questioning enables teachers to translate their curiosity about what students say into probing disciplined questions. By wondering aloud, teachers simultaneously convey interest in and respect for student thought, and model analytical moves for students. Fruitful Socratic discussion infects students with the same curiosity about the meaning of and truth of what they think, hear, and read and gives students the clear message that they are expected to think with discipline and to take everyone else's statements and ideas seriously.

Socratic questioning is based on the idea that all thinking has a logic or structure, that any single statement only partially reveals the thinking underlying it, expressing no more than a tiny piece of the system of interconnected beliefs of which it is a part. Its purpose is to expose the logic of someone's thought. Use of Socratic questioning presupposes the following points: All thinking has assumptions; makes claims or creates meaning; has implications and consequences; focuses on some things and throws others into the background; uses some concepts or ideas and not others; is defined by purposes, issues, or problems; uses or explains some facts and not others; is relatively clear or unclear; is relatively deep or superficial; is relatively critical or uncritical; is relatively elaborated or undeveloped; is relatively mono-logical or multi-logical.

Socratic instruction can take many forms. Socratic questions can come from the teacher or from students. They can be used in a large group discussion, in small groups, one-to-one, or even with oneself. They can have different purposes. What each form has in common is that someone's thought is developed as a result of the probing, stimulating questions asked. It requires questioners to "try on" others' beliefs, to imagine what it would mean to accept them, and to wonder what it would be like to believe otherwise.

If a student says that people are selfish, the teacher may wonder aloud as to what it means to say that, or what the student thinks it means to say that an act or person was unselfish. The discussion which follows should help clarify the concepts of selfish and unselfish behavior, identify the kind of evidence required to determine whether or not someone is or is not acting selfishly, and explore the consequences of accepting or rejecting the original generalization. Such a discussion enables students to examine their own views on such concepts as generosity, motivation, obligation, human nature, and right and wrong.

Some people erroneously believe that holding a Socratic discussion is like conducting a chaotic free-for-all. In fact, Socratic discussion has distinctive goals and distinctive ways to achieve them. Indeed, any discussion—any thinking—guided by Socratic questioning is structured and disciplined. The discussion, the thinking, is structured to take student thought from the unclear to the clear, from the unreasoned to the reasoned, from the implicit to the explicit, from the unexamined to the examined, from the inconsistent to the consistent, from the unarticulated to the articulated. To learn how to participate in it, one has to learn how to listen carefully to what others say, to look for reasons and evidence, to recognize and reflect upon assumptions, to discover implications and consequences, to seek examples, analogies, and objections, to seek to discover, in short, what is really known and to distinguish it from what is merely believed.

## Sources of Student Belief

The teacher who thinks critically about instruction realizes that students have two sources of belief: beliefs that the student forms as a result of personal experience, inward thinking, and interaction with peers and environment; and beliefs that the student learns through instruction by adults (at home and at school).

The first could be called "real" or "operational" beliefs. They are what define the student's real world, the foundation for action, the source of acted-upon values. They result from the student giving meaning to what is happening in the world. These beliefs are heavily influenced by what has been called "pleasure principle thinking." They are in large measure egocentric, sociocentric, unreflective, and unarticulated. Moreover, they represent most of the beliefs held by students and that guide student behavior.

People believe in many things for irrational reasons: because others hold the belief, because certain desires may be justified by the belief, because they feel more comfortable with the belief, because they are rewarded for the belief, because they ego-identify with the belief, because others might reject them for not acting on the belief, because the belief helps to justify feelings of like or dislike toward others.

Students, of course, also have spontaneously formed reasonable beliefs. Thus, the operational beliefs of students contain egocentric, sociocentric, and irrational beliefs, mixed together with rational, reasonable, and sensible beliefs.

Some student beliefs are inconsistent with the expressed beliefs of parents and teachers. Because of this contradiction with authority, students rarely raise their operational beliefs to what Piaget calls "conscious realization." As a rule, students separate what they have come to believe through personal experience from what they "learn" from adults at home and in school. They compartmentalize these two sets of beliefs. Consequently, students do not generally apply what they learn in school to life's issues and problems.

Naturally, the second source of belief, instruction from adult authority figures, is based in the authority's interpretation of reality, not the student's. Because adult thinking can be based in bias, prejudice, self-deception, misunderstanding, and so forth, and because the content we teach in school can be flawed, it cannot be assumed that what is taught in school is either rational or defensible.

Therefore, it is important for students to have opportunities to verbalize the two sets of beliefs, to find harmony or contradictions between them. It is important for them to be given opportunities to identify problems in their own belief systems and the belief systems offered by adults, to synthesize what they learn in one belief system with what they learn in other belief systems. They can do this only in an atmosphere that is mutually supportive and student-centered.

The teacher concerned with this problem, then, provides an environment in which students can discover and explore their beliefs. Such teachers refrain from rushing students who are struggling to express their beliefs. They allow time for thoughtful discussion. They do not allow students to attack one another for their beliefs. They reward students for questioning their own beliefs. They encourage students to consider many points of view, and they invite students to question the viewpoints offered by authority figures (including those of the teacher). They teach students to question anything and everything that seems questionable, and then to assess answers using intellectual standards. One effective way of doing this is by using a disciplined questioning process that helps students uncover what they believe, and then analyze their beliefs for cogency.

Unless the teacher provides conditions in which students can discover operational beliefs through reflective thinking, these two systems of beliefs will exist in separate dimensions of their lives. The first will control their deeds, especially private deeds; the second will control their words, especially public words. The first will be used when acting for themselves, the second when performing for others. Through disciplined questioning, teachers can help students discover, and come to terms with, the inconsistencies within and between these two ways of thinking, can help them explore contradictions, double standards, and hypocrisies in their thoughts and deeds as well as the thoughts and deeds of others, and, through the process, foster fair-minded critical thinking.

## General Guidelines for Socratic Questioning

### Think Along With the Class

There is no good mechanical way to lead a Socratic discussion. You should strive, therefore, to think along with the class as you lead the discussion. In doing so, it is essential that you listen carefully to each and every input into the discussion. Whenever a student responds to a question, you must seriously think about what that student has said and size up what sort of contribution it provides to the discussion. However, for an answer to contribute to the discussion, it must be clear. Do not determine the place of a student comment in the discussion until you are sure you understand what the student is saying. Try to enter the student's point of view before you decide how the student's comment fits in.

### There Are Always A Variety of Ways You Can Respond

Remember, that no matter what a person says or thinks, there are multiple ways to respond to that person's thought. Here are a few possibilities:

- How did you come to believe that?
- Do you have any evidence to support that?
- Does anything in your experience illustrate that?
- If we accept what you are saying, what are some implications?
- How might someone object to that position?

### Do Not Hesitate to Pause and Reflect Quietly

Don't feel that you have to rush in responding to what students say. Good thinking usually takes time. Give yourself—and the students—time to think through what is being said. Be prepared to say things like, "I need a moment to think that through." "That's an interesting thought. I'd like each of you to take a few minutes to think of how you might respond to that point if I called on you. In fact, I need to think for a few minutes to figure out what I might say in response."

### Keep Control of the Discussion

Make sure you enforce discipline in the discussion so that there is only one person who has the floor at any given time, and that everyone pays attention to whatever is said. Model the fact that every comment is given due consideration. Call on students to summarize what other students have said. Do not allow students to simply jump in or to interrupt someone who has the floor.

**Periodically Summarize Where the Discussion Is: What Questions
Have Been Answered; What Questions Are Yet Unresolved**

Because Socratic discussions often cover a variety of angles on a question, and a large variety of remarks are made along the way, students need help in seeing what the discussion has and has not accomplished, what has been settled and what still needs to be figured out. This is where you come in. Periodically summarize what seems to have been settled in the discussion so far and what questions are still unanswered. Or first ask a student to summarize what has been settled, and what is still unanswered. Then you summarize if you think anything has been left out.

### Think Of Yourself As a Kind of Intellectual Orchestra Leader

As the discussion leader, you are functioning like an intellectual orchestra leader. You are ensuring that melody and not cacophony results. You ensure that everyone is following the score, that no one is drowning out anyone else, that the heart of the discussion is maintained. Your questions bring discipline and order to the discussion.

### Keep Control of the Question on the Floor

Realize that the person who asks a question is the one guiding the discussion, because thinking at any given moment is driven by the particular question being addressed. Therefore, make sure you maintain control of the questions being asked during the discussion, or, if you decide to let students ask questions, figure out how you are going to direct the handling of the questions. Keep control of the discussion, ensuring that what is said and done in response to a question advances the overall discussion and the ultimate questions being asked.

### Help Students Transfer What They Learn in Socratic Dialogue From the Public Voice to the Private Inner Voice That Guides Their Behavior

The Socratic discussion leader is to the class what the voice of critical thinking is to the individual mind. In both cases, it is a voice that focuses on thinking carefully through questions. Socratic dialogue creates a public voice. Ultimately, we want our students to internalize this public voice as an inner voice that questions in an explicit and disciplined manner. We want them to begin to Socratically question their own assumptions, inferences and conclusions, to bring probing questions into their basic patterns of thought on an everyday basis, to routinely think about their thinking, to routinely question the answers they are unquestioningly inclined to give.

## Decide When to Wonder Aloud

As you develop your Socratic questioning abilities, you will find yourself wondering in many directions. You will often, however, be unsure about how many of these wonderings to share with your students. You certainly don't want to overwhelm them. Neither do you want to confuse them or lead them in too many directions at once. So when do you make the wonderings explicit in the form of a question and when do you keep them in the privacy of your mind?

There is no pat formula or procedure for answering these questions, though there are some guiding principles:

- **Test and find out.** There is nothing wrong with some of your questions misfiring. You can't always predict the precise questions that will best stimulate student thought. So don't be afraid of trial-and-error questioning.

- **Tie into student experience and perceived needs.** As you formulate questions, focus on connecting academic material to student experience. Where possible, use examples that students find intuitive. Match the level of questioning to the level of student ability.

- **Be perseverant.** If students don't respond to a question, wait. If they still don't respond, you might rephrase the question or break it down into simpler questions.

The level of the questions you ask should match the level of student thought and abilities. It should not be assumed that students will immediately take to it. Nevertheless, properly used, Socratic questioning can be introduced in some form or other at virtually any grade level.

# Part Four

## The Role of Questions in Teaching, Thinking, and Learning

Now that you have an understanding of the mechanics of Socratic questioning and the critical thinking concepts that enrich any Socratic dialogue, we will lay out, in the last two parts of this guide, a substantive concept of Socratic questioning. In developing our concept:

1. We first discuss the critical role that questioning plays in the mind of the educated person, and the importance (therefore) of placing questioning at the heart of the educational process.

2. We review the historical roots of the Socratic method, summarizing the philosophy and questioning practices of Socrates.

3. We link the dialectic method used by Socrates to critical thinking, emphasizing what critical thinking theory contributes to the Socratic questioning process. In other words, we amplify the practice of Socratic questioning by demonstrating the application of critical thinking concepts to it.

## The Teacher as Questioner

Any teacher concerned with the development of the student's mind must be concerned with the role of questions in teaching and learning, for it is through our questions that we understand the world and everything in it. It is through our questions that we understand subject matter and academic disciplines. It is through our questions that we express our intellectual goals and purposes. It is through our questions that we think superficially or deeply.

If we want to foster critical thinking, we must create an environment that is conducive to critical thinking. We must create, within the classroom and school environment, a mini-critical society, a place where the values of critical thinking (truth, open-mindedness, empathy, autonomy, rationality, and self-critique) are encouraged and rewarded. In such an environment, students learn to believe in the power of their own minds to identify and solve problems. They learn to believe in the efficacy of their own thinking. Thinking for themselves is not something they fear. Authorities are not those who tell them the "right" answers, but those who encourage and help them figure out answers for themselves, who encourage them to discover the powerful resources of their own minds. Questions, both those they ask and those the teacher asks, are at the front and center of everything that happens in the classroom.

The teacher is much more a questioner than a preacher in any substantive critical thinking model. The teacher learns how to ask questions that probe meanings, that explore reasons and evidence, that facilitate elaboration, that keep discussions from becoming confusing, that provide incentives for listening to what others have to say, that lead to fruitful comparisons and contrasts, that highlight contradictions and inconsistencies, and that identify implications and consequences. Teachers committed to critical thinking realize that the primary purpose of all education is to *teach students how to learn*. Since there are more details than can be taught and no way to predict which the student will need, teachers emphasize thinking about basic issues and problems. Thus, details are learned as a necessary part of the process of settling questions, and so are functional and relevant.

## Understanding Content as Interrelated Systems With Real-Life Connections

Teachers who foster learning how to learn and who focus on tools for reasoning through issues and problems help students gain knowledge they can use the rest of their lives. These teachers realize that subject matter divisions are arbitrary and a matter of convenience, that the most important problems of everyday life rarely fall neatly into subject matter divisions, that fully understanding a situation usually requires a synthesis of knowledge and insight from several subjects. Hence, an in-depth understanding of one subject requires an understanding of others. (One cannot answer questions in history, for example, without asking and answering related questions in psychology, sociology, and so on.).

Students discover the value of knowledge, evidence, and reasoning by experiencing significant payoffs from them in their everyday life problems outside of school. In other words, they need to see the connection between what they learn in school and how they live their lives. Recognizing the universal problems we all face, the teacher should encourage each student to find reasonable solutions to important questions, questions like:

Who am I? What is the world really like? What are my parents, my friends, and other people like? How have I become the way I am? What should I believe in? Why should I believe in it? What real options do I have? Who are my real friends? Who should I trust? Who are my enemies? Need they be my enemies? How did the world become the way it is? How do people become the way they are? Are there any really bad people in the world? Are there any really good people in the world? What is good and bad? What is right and wrong? How should I decide? How can I decide what is fair and what is unfair? How can I be fair to others? Do I have to be fair to my enemies? How should I live my life? What rights do I have? What responsibilities?

The teacher who believes in personal freedom and thinking for oneself does not spoon-feed students predigested answers to questions. Nor should students be encouraged to believe that all answers are arbitrary and a matter of sheer opinion. To develop their intellects, students must pursue understandings within subjects using their own thinking. They must come to understand content as inherently connected with questions within the discipline, questions that become a source of inquiry for them if they learn to think within the discipline. Moreover, they must learn to reason through questions using skill and discipline. The teacher fosters skilled inquiry by modeling the process, by asking probing questions and by encouraging students to do the same. Neither the discussion nor the student should be forced to conclusions that do not seem reasonable to the student.

Thus, teachers concerned with fostering deep learning think critically about the subjects they teach. They routinely reflect upon questions such as:

What ideas and skills are the most basic and crucial in this subject? What do practitioners in this field do? How do they think? Why should students be familiar with this subject? What use does a well-educated person and citizen of a republic make of this subject? How can these uses be made apparent to and real for my students? Where do the various subject areas overlap? How should the tools and insights of each subject inform one's understanding of the others? Of one's place in the world?

One of the problems in schooling is that teachers tend to overemphasize "coverage" over "engaged thinking." One of the reasons for this is that they do not fully appreciate the role of questions in teaching content. Consequently, they assume that answers can be taught separate from questions. Indeed, so buried are questions in established instruction that the fact that all assertions—all statements that this or that is so—are implicit answers to questions is virtually never recognized. For example, the statement that water boils at 100 degrees centigrade is an answer to the question "At what temperature centigrade does water boil?" Hence, every declarative statement in the textbook is an answer to a question. Hence, every textbook could be rewritten in the interrogative mode by translating every statement into a question. To our knowledge this has never been done. That it has not is testimony to the privileged status of *answers* over *questions* in instruction and the fact that teachers tend to misunderstand the significance of questions in the learning process. In most instruction today, the majority of the questions at the heart of the disciplines are buried in a torrent of obscured "answers."

## Thinking is Driven By Questions

However, thinking is not driven by answers but by questions. Had no questions been asked by those who laid the foundation for a field—for example, Physics or Biology—the field would never have developed in the first place. Furthermore, every field stays alive only to the extent that fresh questions are generated and taken seriously as the driving force in a process of thinking. To think through or rethink anything, one must ask questions that stimulate thought.

Questions define tasks, express problems, and delineate issues. Answers on the other hand, often signal a full stop in thought. Only when an answer generates a further question does thought continue its life as such. This is why it is true that only when students have questions are they really thinking and learning. It is possible to give students an examination on any subject by just asking them to list all of the questions that they have about a subject, including all questions generated by their first list of questions. That we do not test students by asking them to list questions and explain the significance of those questions is again evidence of the privileged status we give to answers isolated from questions. That is, we tend to ask questions only to get thought-stopping answers, not to generate further questions.

Feeding students endless content to remember (that is, declarative sentences to remember) is akin to repeatedly stepping on the brakes in a vehicle that is, unfortunately, already at rest. Instead, students need questions to turn on their intellectual engines. They need to generate questions from our questions to get their thinking to go somewhere. Thinking is of no use unless it goes somewhere, and again, the questions we ask determine where our thinking goes.

Deep questions drive our thought underneath the surface of things, forcing us to deal with complexities. Questions of purpose force us to define our task. Questions of information force us to look at our sources of information as well as at the quality of our information. Questions of interpretation force us to examine how we are organizing or giving meaning to information. Questions of assumption force us to examine what we are taking for granted. Questions of implication force us to follow out where our thinking is going. Questions of point of view force us to examine our point of view and to consider other relevant points of view.

Questions of relevance force us to discriminate what does and what does not bear on a question. Questions of accuracy force us to evaluate and test for truth and correctness. Questions of precision force us to give details and be specific. Questions of consistency force us to examine our thinking for contradictions. Questions of logic force us to consider how we are putting the whole of our thought together, to make sure that it all adds up and makes sense within a reasonable system of some kind.

Unfortunately, most students ask virtually none of these thought-stimulating types of questions. They tend to stick to dead questions like "Is this going to be on the test?," questions that imply the desire not to think. Most teachers in turn are not themselves generators of questions and answers of their own. They are not seriously engaged in thinking through or rethinking through their own subjects. Rather, they are purveyors of the questions and answers of others—usually those of a textbook.

We must continually remind ourselves that thinking begins within some content area only when teachers and students generate questions within the content. No questions equals no understanding. Superficial questions equals superficial understanding.

Most students typically have no questions. They not only sit in silence, their minds are silent as well. Hence, the questions they do ask tend to be superficial and ill formed. This demonstrates that most of the time they are not thinking through the content they are presumed to be learning.

If we want productive and effective thinking to occur in the minds of our students, we must stimulate student thinking with questions that lead them to further questions. We must overcome what previous schooling has done to their thinking. We must resuscitate minds that are largely inert when we receive them. We must give our students what might be called "artificial cogitation" (the intellectual equivalent of artificial respiration).

It is important for students to learn, as they develop their questioning abilities, that no thought is ever "complete" in itself, but is always open to further development. Understanding thinking itself is also incomplete. From this insight emerges *intellectual humility* on the part of the reflective student, the awareness of the limitations of human thought and understanding, the awareness that thinking (driven by questions) is always at such and such a stage of development. In principle, it can never be complete.

Thus, questioning in a healthy mind never ends. Questions become transformed and enriched. They move thought on and on until the thinker is satisfied and stops. Answers are merely places to rest for a moment. They are not final. There is always an unlimited network of paths of further possible thinking that can yet be followed.

# Part Five

## Socrates, the Socratic Method, and Critical Thinking

To question well, and therefore to think well, we need tools for questioning. We need to know how to question. We need skills of inquiry that enable us to ask fruitful and productive questions that guide our thinking to fruitful and productive answers. In short, we need Socratic questioning abilities.

In this section, we explore the concept of Socratic questioning as a disciplined, systematic form of questioning. We focus first on the historical roots of the Socratic method as developed and exhibited by Socrates. We then define critical thinking, and link it to Socratic questioning, elaborating on the importance of critical thinking to effective Socratic questioning.

### A Definition of Socratic Questioning

To formulate our concept of Socratic questioning, let us first consider several related definitions. We will then bring together the insights within these definitions.

The terms *Socratic dialogue* and *dialectic* are often used interchangeably. Consider the following two definitions found in *Webster's New World Dictionary, Second College Edition* (1986):

**Socratic method.** The dialectic method of teaching or discussion used by Socrates, involving the asking of a series of easily answered questions that inevitably lead the answerer to a logical conclusion foreseen by the questioner.

**Dialectic.** The art or practice of examining opinions or ideas logically, often by the method of question and answer, to determine their validity.

Now consider these same terms as found in *Webster's Encyclopedic Unabridged Dictionary of the English Language* (1989). As you will see, they are viewed from a slightly different angle:

**Socratic method.** The use of questions, as employed by Socrates, to develop a latent idea, as in the mind of a pupil, or to elicit admissions, as from an opponent, tending to establish a proposition.

**Dialectic.** The art or practice of logical discussion as employed in investigating the truth of a theory or opinion.

Note that there are at least two key terms within this second definition of *Socratic method* that may need further explication. Again, we find the following definitions in *Webster's Encyclopedic Unabridged Dictionary of the English Language* (1989):

**Latent.** Present, but not visual, apparent, or actualized; existing as potential.

**Proposition.** Anything stated or affirmed for discussion or illustration; a statement in which something is affirmed or denied so that it can therefore be characterized as true or false.

If we take into account all of these definitions, we might define Socratic questioning in this way:

The art of asking questions and pursing answers, originated by Socrates (Athens, Third and Fourth Century BC), that aims at one or more of the following:

1. Investigating the truth of a theory or opinion.
2. Eliciting and developing an idea present in the mind but not yet developed or actualized.
3. Leading the answerer to a logical or valid conclusion, either foreseen or unforeseen by the questioner.
4. Eliciting admission, on the part of an opponent, of a statement or conclusion that can then be examined for truth or falsity.

## On Socrates

With this definition in mind, let us look briefly at the life of Socrates, focusing especially on his questioning abilities, skills, and dispositions. This will enable us to outline the dialectic mode of questioning that has become known as the *Socratic Method*.

Socrates was an early Greek philosopher and teacher (c. 470–399 BC) who believed that the best way to teach and learn was through disciplined, rigorous questioning. In other words, he thought that people learned best, not by being told what to believe or do, but by being guided through questioning to what made most sense to believe or do. He often used questioning to help people see either that what they said they believed they did not, in fact, believe (because their "beliefs" were inconsistent with their behavior), or that what they said they believed was conceptually unsound or illogical.

When questioning others, Socrates often functioned as both teacher and student, modeling the kind of disciplined inquiry he thought people needed to engage in if they were to live a rational life. Consider:

> Socrates philosophized by joining in a discussion with another person who thought he knew what justice, courage, or the like was. Under Socrates' questioning, it became clear that neither [of the two] knew, and they cooperated in a new effort, Socrates making interrogatory suggestions that were accepted or rejected by his friend. They failed to solve the problem, but, now conscious of their lack of knowledge, agreed to continue the search whenever possible. These discussions, or "dialectics," whereby Socrates engaged in his question-and-answer investigations, were…the very marrow of the Socratic legacy *(Encyclopedia of Philosophy,* 1972, p. 483).

Socrates also used questioning when dealing with his adversaries, revealing, through the pursuit of answers to questions he formulated, that their reasoning was illogical, unsound, or otherwise unjustifiable.

Socrates was fundamentally concerned with the *soundness of reasoning,* with getting closer and closer to the truth in any given situation. He was more interested in *the process of learning,* for him, the questioning process, than in reaching conclusions. He was at home with complexities, confusion, perplexities, and uncertainties. He was known for the sharpness of his mind, the ways in which he opened up questions for debate and discussion, and the seemingly tireless source of energy he expended in expanding his mind— and helping others do the same.

Because there are no written works by Socrates upon which we can rely, we know little about his thoughts or philosophy first hand. What we do know about him comes primarily from the work of two of his students, Plato and Xenophon (although many others wrote about Socrates—both during his lifetime and after his death).

In Athens, in 399 BC, Socrates was accused, indicted, and ultimately put to death for two reasons:

1.  Introducing and believing in gods other than those sanctioned by the state. (Although some accused Socrates of atheism, all evidence points in the opposite direction, evidenced, in part, by the fact that Socrates believed in life after death.)

2.  Corrupting the young (by fostering their intellectual development, and encouraging them to question the status quo).

To understand the philosophy and influence of Socrates, it is useful to consider the question, "To what extent was Socrates in fact a threat to the State?"

There was reason for fearing Socrates as a social force. Where arête [excellence, in terms of how to make the best of oneself and live a rational life], education, and state were fused in one image, an educator critical of received assumptions was a revolutionary. Socrates not only publicly raised such fundamental questions as "What is arête?" and "Who are its teachers?" but also by discrediting through their own representatives the accepted educational channels and by creating a climate of questioning and doubt, he was suspected by conservative minds of the dangerous game of discomfiting all authority before a circle of impressionable youths and subtracting from the state the stability of tradition. It was also apparent that the values by which Socrates lived, his indifference to material wealth and prosperity, and his freedom from desire and ambition were themselves a living criticism of all institutions and of politicians who did not seem to know what they were doing or who were compromising their principles (p. 482). Socrates was perhaps the most original, influential, and controversial figure in the history of Greek thought…he was obviously at home in the best society, but he had no respect for social status…he fell to a level of comparative poverty, which was in tune with his arguments on the unimportance of material goods and his own simple needs… Tradition holds that by refusing to compromise his principles, he deliberately antagonized the court which was trying him for impiety and forced an avoidable death penalty *(The Encyclopedia of Philosophy,* 1972, p. 480).

## The Intellectual Virtues as Displayed by Socrates

It is important to recognize the intellectual virtues or traits Socrates routinely exhibited, the development of which can come only through years of committed practice. First, and perhaps most important, he was a living example of intellectual humility. He was keenly aware of the limits of his knowledge, and was quite comfortable pointing out those limits to others—a rare human quality. In fact, he recognized his weaknesses as a strength, as a first step to understanding. Socrates also believed that the primary reason people behave irrationally is because they lack knowledge of the rational way to behave. In his book, *A History of Western Philosophy*, Bertrand Russell[2] comments on this point:

> The Platonic Socrates consistently maintains that he knew nothing, and is only wiser than others in knowing that he knows nothing, but he does not think knowledge unobtainable. On the contrary, he thinks the search for knowledge of the utmost importance. He maintains that no man sins wittingly, and therefore only knowledge is needed to make all men perfectly virtuous (p. 92).

The entry on Socrates in the *Encyclopedia Britannica*, Eleventh Edition (1911), supports this view, portraying Socrates as a person not only of intellectual humility, but of intellectual autonomy as well:

> Profoundly sensible of the inconsistencies of his own thoughts and words and actions, and shrewdly suspecting that the like inconsistencies were to be found in other men, he was careful always to place himself upon the standpoint of ignorance and to invite others to join him there, in order that, proving all things, he and they might hold fast to that which is good (p. 332). When experience showed that those who esteemed themselves wise were unable to give an account of their knowledge, he had to admit that…he was wiser than the others, in so far as, whilst they, being ignorant, supposed themselves to know, he, being ignorant, was aware of his ignorance (p. 333).

> [Socrates had] a real greatness of soul, a hearty and unaffected disregard of public opinion…and entire abnegation of self. He made himself a fool that others by his folly might be made wise; he humbled himself to the level of those among whom his work lay, that he might raise some few among them to his own level; he was all things to all men, if by any means he might win some (p 333).

When working with students, Socrates often feigned ignorance on a particular issue or topic, and then tried to elicit, through a line of questioning, the full extent of students' knowledge. He wanted his students to come to see, during the dialectic process, problems inherent in their conceptualizations and assumptions, contradictions in their thoughts and behavior. He wanted to exhibit, in himself, a model of intellectual humility and autonomy for students to emulate.

Socrates attempted to foster in his students the ability to formulate a *disciplined line of questioning*, to think within new perspectives and viewpoints, to uncover biases and distortions. Most of all, he wanted his students to develop a passion for examining ideas and ferreting out the truth. He exhibited and cultivated **confidence in reason**, believing that the pursuit of knowledge is the primary function of human thought, and should be pursued rigorously and routinely in everyday life. He thought that any idea that could not stand the test of sound reasoning and judgment should and must be abandoned.

Socrates exhibited **intellectual perseverance**, pursuing ideas and questions with energy and zest, infecting others with his delight in learning, never tiring of the process. Consistently attempting to live in accordance with the ideals he espoused, and never

---

2 Russell, B. 1972. *A History of Western Philosophy*, NY, NY: Simon & Schuster.

afraid to stand alone in his views, as long as those views had been rigorously analyzed and assessed, Socrates was a living example of both **intellectual integrity** and intellectual autonomy. And through **intellectual courage**, he was willing to face an angry mob of accusers at his trial and to stand alone in his views, views that had been developed with discipline and rigor throughout a lifetime, even when facing the probability of a death sentence.

## The Systematic Nature of the Socratic Method

Socrates was concerned with developing a systematic method of disciplined questioning that could be emulated. By studying the Socratic dialogues, we can explicate the components and processes that came to be known as the Socratic method. In fact, if we are to emulate the intellectual skills and dispositions of Socrates, it is important to delineate, as clearly and precisely as we can, the dialectic method he advocated. This method can be outlined as follows:

1. **The best way to teach is through dialectic reasoning, primarily through a question-and-answer process.** This method of learning enables students to practice, through many years, pursuing answers to questions in a rigorous, methodical way. Disciplined questioning should focus on a specific foundational concept or question, and should include a careful use of analogies intuitive to the "student."

2. **There are two primary processes required for replacing faulty thinking with sound thinking—the destructive and the constructive process.** In the destructive process, ideas formerly held dear to the student are shown to be illogical or otherwise unsound. In other words, the student comes to recognize the flawed nature of his reasoning. In the constructive process, the student is encouraged to replace the flawed thinking with logical or justifiable thinking.

3. **The teacher should help students uncover self-deception in their thinking.** (This makes evident the fact that Socrates was aware of the self-deceptive nature of human thought—and the tremendous problem of self-deception in human life.)

4. **A primary goal of the teacher should be to help students formulate principles by which to live,** principles that emerge out of deep conceptual understandings.

## Placing the Dialectic Process at the Heart of Teaching

Socrates viewed education, properly so called, as a complex process requiring active disciplined engagement in learning. In his view, the only way students can learn important and meaningful ideas is through engaging their minds *intellectually*. Therefore, the role of the teacher is to foster intellectual discipline and skill. He thought that the best way to foster the development of deep and important insights was, not by telling students what to do or think, nor by giving them information that would lie dormant in the mind, but through a question-and-answer method, wherein students were, in essence, forced to engage their minds in thinking through a complex concept or issue.

In fact, Socrates believed that teachers did not have the right to force their views or opinions on their students. He considered the question-and-answer process to be the *only* defensible instructional method.

> Though he had neither the right, nor the power, to force his opinions upon another, he might, by a systematic interrogatory lead another to substitute a better opinion for a worse, just as a physician, by appropriate remedies, may enable his patient to substitute a healthy sense of taste for a morbid one. When he described himself as a "talker" or "converser,"...[he] positively indicated the method of question and answer which he consistently preferred and habitually practiced. It was in this way that Socrates was brought to regard "dialectic," "question and answer," as the only admissible method of education *(Encyclopedia Britannica,* Eleventh Edition, 1911, p. 335).

## The Historical Contribution of Socrates

Socrates was fundamentally concerned with the practical issue of helping people *develop the reasoning abilities requisite to living a rational life.* Recognizing the importance of rational thought to rational decisions and behavior, and yet the pervasive lack of rationality in human thought, Socrates worked tirelessly to help people discover the link between how they thought and how they lived.

Though several of his students attempted to capture the system of questioning Socrates modeled, and though the Socratic dialogues are still widely read today, the influence of Socrates on human thought and deed seems minimal at best.

Nevertheless, the Socratic method, as emulated by Socrates, offers a systematic, disciplined approach to questioning. It offers an approach that, when integrated with critical thinking concepts and principles, provides us with a rich set of intellectual tools which can guide us to deeper and deeper levels of understanding, which can lead us beneath the self-deceptive cover for irrational thinking, which can lead us to greater and ever more important truths.

Let us now turn to the concept of critical thinking, first laying out a definition, and then considering the relationship between critical thinking and the Socratic method.

## The Concept of Critical Thinking

The concept of critical thinking reflects an idea derived from roots in ancient Greek. The word "critical" derives etymologically from two Greek roots: kriticos (meaning discerning judgment) and kriterion (meaning standards). Etymologically, then, the word implies the development of "discerning judgment based on standards." In *Webster's New World Dictionary,* the relevant entry for "critical" reads "characterized by careful analysis and judgment" and is followed by: "Critical, in its strictest sense, implies an attempt at objective judgment so as to determine both merits and faults." Considering these definitions together, then, critical thinking may be appropriately defined as:

> Thinking explicitly aimed at well-founded judgment, utilizing appropriate evaluative standards in an attempt to determine the true worth, merit, or value of something.

Critical thinking, then, has three dimensions: an analytic, an evaluative, and a creative component. As a critical thinker, we analyze thinking in order to evaluate it. We evaluate it in order to improve it.

In other words, critical thinking is the *systematic monitoring of thought with the end goal of improvement.* When we think critically, we realize that thinking must not be accepted at face value, but must be analyzed and assessed for its *clarity, accuracy, relevance, depth, breadth, and logicalness.* We recognize that all reasoning occurs within *points of view* and frames of reference, that all reasoning proceeds from some *goals and objectives* and has an *informational base,* that all data when used in reasoning must be *interpreted,* that interpretation involves *concepts,* that concepts entail *assumptions,* and that all basic inferences in thought have *implications.* Because problems in thinking can occur in any of these dimensions, each dimension must be monitored.

When we think critically, we realize that in every domain of human thought, it is possible and important to question the parts of thinking using the standards for thought. Routine questioning in the critical mind involves disciplined questioning as suggested by, but not limited to, the following:

Let's see, what is the most fundamental issue here? From what point of view should I approach this problem? Does it make sense for me to assume this? What may I reasonably infer from these data? What is implied in this graph? What is the fundamental concept here? Is this information consistent with that information? What makes this question complex? How could I check the accuracy of these data? If this is so, what else is implied? Is this a credible source of information?

With intellectual language such as this in the foreground, one can come to recognize fundamental critical thinking "moves" that can be used in reasoning through any problem or issue, class or subject.

When we learn the language of critical thinking, we can then use the language in formulating and asking questions. With the analytic and evaluative tools of critical thinking, we raise the quality of the questions we can ask.

## What Critical Thinking Brings to Socratic Questioning

Socrates, almost by nature, questioned what seemed to him to be illogical, inaccurate, or unsound; and he questioned with skill and expertise. After many years of practice, questioning was deeply intrinsic to his character. Although he attempted to develop a system of questioning, that system was not altogether made explicit. It does not appear that he had a precisely developed theory underlying the questioning process he advocated. In other words, if we were to analyze the specific questions Socrates asked at specific points in his dialogues, we may find it difficult to emulate in our own questioning process the "intellectual moves" he was making. We might ask, for example, how he decided to ask a particular question at a given point, what concepts or assumptions drove him to the next question, how he determined which direction to take. In support of this point, it is interesting to note that, although Socrates had many students throughout his lifetime, few are said to have the power of questioning he possessed.

This well may be true because, although Socrates was highly skilled at questioning, his students did not easily emulate the types of questions he asked at any given point in a discussion. In other words, his skill in questioning seems to have been *implicit*, rather than *explicit*, perhaps even for him.

Critical thinking, on the other hand, provides us with *definitive and specific tools* for questioning. There is nothing mysterious about the most basic ideas in critical thinking that can and should be applied to formulating and asking questions, and that should be fostered in the thinking of all students. For example, through critical thinking, we learn that *all thinking has a purpose.* When students understand this, they can ask questions which focus on explicating purposes. So they can ask questions such as: "What is your purpose for doing what you just did? What is the purpose in this assignment? What is the purpose of college? What is the purpose of government?" and so on, focusing on any purpose within any situation. Moreover, when they have identified the purpose in a situation, they can take the next step in thinking—assessing the purpose.

Critical thinking, then, is the *key* to Socratic questioning because it makes the intellectual moves used in Socratic dialogue explicit and accessible to anyone interested in learning it, and willing to practice it.

# Appendix A

## Patterns in Teaching that Incorporate Socratic Dialogue

Every teacher teaches in a patterned way, though few teachers are explicitly aware of the patterns implicit in their teaching. For many teachers, the pattern consists in nothing more than this: lecture, lecture, lecture, quiz; lecture, lecture, lecture, quiz; lecture, lecture, lecture, mid-term exam, with occasional question and answer periods focused on recalling information from lectures and textbooks. It is important for teachers to examine their instruction, looking for patterns, to critique those patterns, and to begin to experiment with patterns that enable them more readily to cultivate the critical thinking of their students. For one thing, once teachers discover one or two powerful patterns of teaching, it is possible to structure a whole semester of teaching around that pattern.

There are many ways in which Socratic Dialogue can be used in conjunction with other effective teaching strategies. In this appendix we lay out three possible schemas for doing so. Within each schema we incorporate a content-based example.

## Schema One

For a lesson on discrimination: The main objective is to have students engage in ethical reasoning. We might use the following pattern:

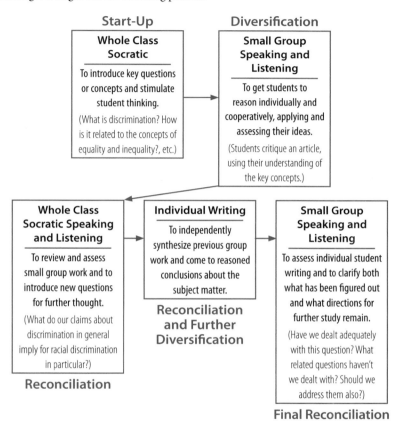

## Schema Two

For a lesson on the civil war: The main objective of this lesson is to teach students how researching historical events can lead us to a better understanding of them, and how this in turn can lead one to benefit from that understanding. We might use the following pattern:

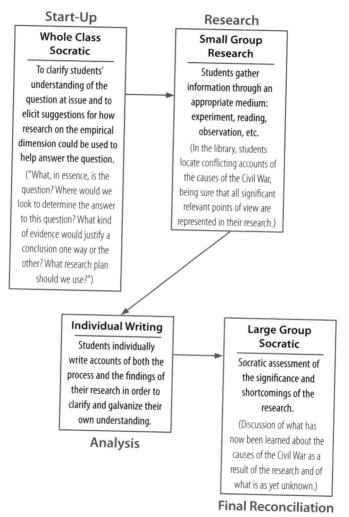

**Start-Up**

**Whole Class Socratic**

To clarify students' understanding of the question at issue and to elicit suggestions for how research on the empirical dimension could be used to help answer the question.

("What, in essence, is the question? Where would we look to determine the answer to this question? What kind of evidence would justify a conclusion one way or the other? What research plan should we use?")

**Research**

**Small Group Research**

Students gather information through an appropriate medium: experiment, reading, observation, etc.

(In the library, students locate conflicting accounts of the causes of the Civil War, being sure that all significant relevant points of view are represented in their research.)

**Individual Writing**

Students individually write accounts of both the process and the findings of their research in order to clarify and galvanize their own understanding.

**Analysis**

**Large Group Socratic**

Socratic assessment of the significance and shortcomings of the research.

(Discussion of what has now been learned about the causes of the Civil War as a result of the research and of what is as yet unknown.)

**Final Reconciliation**

## Schema Three

For a lesson on critical reading: The main objective of the lesson is to help students gain skill in critical reading through practice.

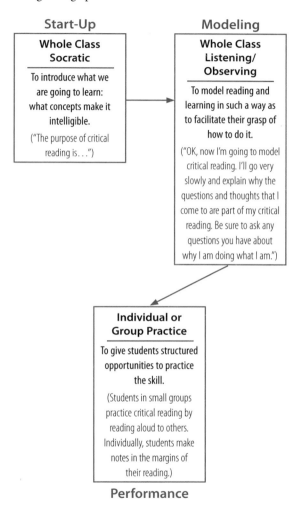

## Start-Up

**Whole Class Socratic**

To introduce what we are going to learn: what concepts make it intelligible.

("The purpose of critical reading is. . .")

## Modeling

**Whole Class Listening/ Observing**

To model reading and learning in such a way as to facilitate their grasp of how to do it.

("OK, now I'm going to model critical reading. I'll go very slowly and explain why the questions and thoughts that I come to are part of my critical reading. Be sure to ask any questions you have about why I am doing what I am.")

**Individual or Group Practice**

To give students structured opportunities to practice the skill.

(Students in small groups practice critical reading by reading aloud to others. Individually, students make notes in the margins of their reading.)

## Performance

# Appendix B

## Analyzed Transcript of a Socratic Dialogue from Plato's Euthyphro

What follows is an excerpt from Plato's *Euthyphro*. This is a dialogue between Socrates and Euthyphro, in which Socrates is questioning Euthyphro on what it means to be pious (and, by implication, what it means to be impious). Through this excerpt, we get a good idea of the basic approach taken by Socrates when questioning others. At the heart of most Socratic dialogues is a concept that is both abstract and deep. Socrates pretends that he doesn't understand the concept, and that he needs help from the person he is questioning in understanding the concept clearly and accurately.

This dialogue takes place outside the courthouse where Socrates is shortly to stand trial. There he meets Euthyphro, "a seer and religious expert, who says that he is going to charge his own father with manslaughter. Socrates is startled, and inquires how Euthyphro can be sure that such conduct is consistent with his religious duty. The result is a discussion of the true nature of Piety. Euthyphro does not represent Athenian orthodoxy; on the contrary, he is sympathetic towards Socrates. He is an independent specialist, confident in his own fallibility, and therefore a fit subject for Socrates' curative treatment, which aims at clearing the mind of false assumptions and so making it receptive of real knowledge…although the argument moves in a circle, it offers clues for the solution of the problem."

What we want most to notice in this, and indeed any dialogue led by Socrates, is how Socrates guides the discussion. We want to understand the precise intellectual moves, if you will, Socrates makes at each point along the way, so that we might emulated those moves. The best way to do this is to use the language of critical thinking to label those moves. As you read through this dialogue, notice the notes we provide relevant to this point (in parentheses and italics). We begin shortly after the beginning of the dialogue, and include a good portion, but not all, of the dialogue.

**Euthyphro:** The man who is dead was a poor dependent of mine who worked for us as a field laborer at Naxos, and one day in a fit of drunken passion he got into a quarrel with one of our domestic servants and slew him. My father bound him hand and foot and threw him into a ditch, and then sent to Athens, to ask of a diviner what he should do with him. Meantime he had no care or thought of him, being under the impression that he was a murderer; and that even if he did die there would be no great harm. And this was just what happened. For such was the effect of cold and hunger and chains upon him, that before the messenger returned from the diviner, he was dead. And my father and family are angry with me for taking the part of the murderer and prosecuting my father. They say that he did not kill him, and if he did, the dead man was but a murderer, and I ought not to take any notice, for that a son is impious who prosecutes a father. That shows,

Socrates, how little they know of the opinions of the gods about piety and impiety.

**Socrates: And what is piety, and what is impiety?**
*(Socrates asks Euthyphro to explicitly state the fundamental difference between two concepts. This is an important early step in conceptual analysis.)*

E: Piety is doing as I am doing; that is to say, prosecuting any one who is guilty of murder, sacrilege, or of any other similar crime—whether he be your father or mother, or some other person, makes no difference—and not persecuting them is impiety. And please to consider, Socrates, what a notable proof I will give you of the truth of what I am saying, which I have already given to others—of the truth, I mean of the principle that the impious, whoever he may be, ought not to go unpunished. For do men regard Zeus as the best and most righteous of the gods?—and even they admit that he bound his father (Cronos) because he wickedly devoured his sons, and that he too has punished his own father (Uranus) for a similar reason, in a nameless manner. And yet when I proceed against my father, they are angry with me. This is their inconsistent way of talking when the gods are concerned, and when I am concerned.

S: *May not this be the reason, Euthyphro, why I am charged with impiety—that I can not away with these stories about the gods? And therefore I suppose that people think me wrong. But, as you who are well informed about them approve of them, I cannot do better than assent to your superior wisdom. For what else can I say, confessing as I do, that I know nothing of them? I wish you would tell me whether you really believe that they are true.*
*(Here, Socrates is saying that Euthyphro, since he purports to know a lot about the gods, should tell Socrates of his knowledge. Socrates refers to the indictment against him—that he believes in gods different from those sanctioned by the state. Socrates is demonstrating intellectual humility, while imlying that Euthyphro is intellectually arrogant in purporting to know what the gods believe.)*

E: Yes, Socrates; and things more wonderful still, of which the world is in ignorance.

S: *And do you really believe that the gods fought with one another, and had dire quarrels, battles, and the like, as the poets say, and as you may see represented in the works of great artists? The temples are full of them. Are all these tales of the gods true, Euthyphro?*

*(Socrates is now directing Euthyphro to think about whether the stories one hears of the gods can be logical.)*

E:  Yes Socrates, and, as I was saying, I can tell you, if you would like to hear them, many other things about the gods which would quite amaze you.

S:  *I dare say; and you shall tell me them at some other time when I have leisure. But just at present I would rather hear from you a more precise answer, which you have not as yet given, my friend, to the question, What is "piety?" In reply you only say that piety is, doing as you do, charging your father with murder?*

*(Note that Socrates is using two intellectual standards in his last comment—he is asking for a "more precise answer," and in doing so, he is redirecting the dialogue back to what is relevant. He is pointing out that an example is not a definition, that if someone asks for a definition, an example does not complete the intellectual task.)*

E:  And that is true, Socrates.

S:  *I dare say, Euthyphro, but there are many other pious acts.*

E:  There are.

S:  *Remember that I did not ask you to give me two or three examples of piety, but to explain the general idea which makes all pious things to be pious. Do you not recollect that there was one idea which made the impious impious, and the pious pious?*

*(Here Socrates is again asking for Euthyphro's definition of pious in order to determine whether his definition is reasonable. He wants Euthyphro to stay focused on the task.)*

E:  I remember.

S:  *Tell me what this is, and then I shall have a standard to which I may look, and by which I may measure the nature of actions, whether yours or any one's else, and say that this action is pious, and that impious?*

*(Socrates is implying that once he has a clear definition of pious, then he can use that definition to determine whether anything is or is not pious. He refers to this as a "standard" by which he can judge.)*

E:  I will tell you, if you like.

S:  *I should very much like.*

E:  Piety, then, is that which is dear to the gods, and impiety is that which is not dear to them.

S:  *Come, then, and let us examine what we are saying, that thing or person which is dear to the gods is pious, and that thing or person which is hateful to the gods is impious. Was not that said? And further, Euthyphro, the gods were admitted to have enmities and hatreds and differences—that was also said?*

*(Socrates is pointing out a fatal flaw in Euthyphro's definition of pious—that anything which is dear to the gods is inherently good—by reminding him that the gods sometimes disagree and fight among themselves. If they were always in agreement about what is pious, they wouldn't fight among themselves.)*

E: Yes, that was said.

S: *And what sort of difference creates enmity and anger? Suppose for example that you and I, my good friend, differ about a number; do differences of this sort make us enemies and set us at variance with one another? Do we not go at once to calculation, and end them by a sum?*

E: True.

S: *Or suppose that we differ about magnitudes, do we not quickly put an end to that difference by measuring?*

E: That is true.

S: *And we end a controversy about heavy and light by resorting to a weighing-machine?*

E: To be sure.

S: *But what difference are those which, because they can not be thus decided, make us angry and set us at enmity with one another? I dare say the answer does not occur to you at the moment, and therefore I will suggest that this happens when the matters of difference are the just and unjust, good and evil, honorable and dishonorable. Are not these the points about which, when differing, and unable satisfactorily to decide our differences, we quarrel, when we do quarrel, as you and I and all men experience? (Socrates at this point is trying to get Euthyphro to see that people are passionate about deep and complex issues, not issues that can easily be answered—and specifically that they often disagree about what is right and wrong about ethics.)*

E: Yes, Socrates, that is the nature of the differences about which we quarrel.

S: *And the quarrels of the gods, noble Euthyphro, when they occur, are of a like nature?*

E: They are.

S: *They have differences of opinion, as you say, about good and evil, just and unjust, honorable and dishonorable: there would have been no quarrels among them, if there had been no such difference—would there now?*

E: You are quite right.

S: *Does not every man love that which he deems noble and just and good, and hate the opposite of them?*

E: Very true.

  www.criticalthinking.org

S: **But then, as you say, people regard the same things, some as just and others as unjust; and they dispute about this and there arise wars and fightings among them.**

E: Yes, this is true.

S: **Then the same things, as appears, are hated by the gods and loved by the gods, and are both hateful and dear to them?**
*(Again, Socrates is making the conceptual point that what is loved by some gods is hated by others, and therefore, you cannot simply say that what is pious is that which the gods love—because they love different, and often the opposite, things, and they despise different, and often opposite, things. He is trying to point out that this definition of pious will not suffice because it is self-contradictory.)*

E: True.

S: **Then upon this view the same things, Euthyphro, will be pious and also impious?**

E: That, I suppose, is true.

S: **Then, my friend, I remark with surprise that you have not answered what I asked. For I certainly did not ask what was that which is at once pious and impious: and that which is loved by the gods appears also to be hated by them. And therefore, Euthyphro, in thus chastising your father you may very likely be doing what is agreeable to Zeus but disagreeable to Cronos or Uranus, and what is acceptable to Hephaestus but unacceptable to Here, and there may be other gods who have similar differences of opinion.**

E: But I believe, Socrates, that all the gods would be agreed as to the propriety of punishing a murderer: there would be no difference of opinion about that.

S: **Well, but speaking of men, Euthyphro, did you ever hear any one arguing that a murderer or any sort of evil-doer ought to be let off?**

E: I should rather say that they are always arguing this, especially in courts of law: they commit all sorts of crimes, and there is nothing that they will not do or say in order to escape punishment.

S: **But do they admit their guilt, Euthyphro, and yet say that they ought not to be punished?**

E: No, they do not.

S: **Then there are some things which they do not venture to say and do: for they do not venture to argue that the guilty are to be unpunished, but they deny their guilt, do they not?**
*(Here, Socrates is saying that people do not usually disagree about what should be punished when it comes to murder or similar "evils." Rather,*

*they disagree about their own guilt in a matter. In other words, Socrates is trying to get Euthyphro to see that there is an essence to the concept of "evil" that everyone would agree to, though they would apply the concept differently in different cases.)*

E: Yes.

S: *And the gods are in the same case, if as you imply they quarrel about [what is] just and unjust, and some of them say that they wrong one another, and others of them deny this. For surely neither God nor man will ever venture to say that the doer of evil is not to be punished: —you don't mean to tell me that?*

E: That is true, Socrates, in the main.

S: *But they join issue about particulars, and this applies not only to men but to the gods; if they dispute at all they dispute about some act which is called in question, and which some affirm to be just, others to be unjust. Is not that true?*

*(Again, Socrates is trying to show that, though people, and gods, might argue about specific cases, they would not argue about the essence of a concept. And he wants Euthyphro to give him the essence of pious, and, conversely, impious.)*

E: Quite true.

S: *Well then, my dear friend Euthyphro, do tell me, for my better instruction and information, what proof have you that in the opinion of all the gods a servant who is guilty of murder, and is put in chains by the master of the dead man, and dies because he is put in chains before his corrector can learn from the interpreters what he ought to do with him, dies unjustly; and that on behalf of such an one a son ought to proceed against his father and accuse him of murder. How would you show that all the gods absolutely agree in approving of his act? Prove to me that, and I will applaud your wisdom as long as you live.*

*(Socrates wants Euthyphro to see that, because the gods disagree on what behavior is commendable, and what is evil, they would not agree on this particular case either, so that using the standard "agreed upon by the gods" to determine what is pious is not a standard one should use to judge whether something is pious or not pious.)*

E: That would not be an easy task, although I could make the matter very clear indeed to you.

S: *I understand; you mean to say that I am not so quick of apprehension as the judges: for to them you will be sure to prove that the act is unjust, and hateful to the gods.*

E: Yes, indeed, Socrates; at least if they will listen to me.

S: *But they will be sure to listen if they find that you are a good speaker.*
*There was a notion that came into my mind while you were speaking; I*
*said to myself: "Well, and what if Euthyphro does prove to me that all the*
*gods regarded the death of the serf as unjust, how do I know anything more*
*of the nature of piety and impiety? For granting that this action may be*
*hateful to the gods, still these distinctions have no bearing on the definition*
*of piety and impiety, for that which is hateful to the gods has been shown*
*to be also pleasing and dear to them." And therefore Euthyphro, I don't ask*
*you to prove this; I will suppose, if you like, that all the gods condemn and*
*abominate such an action. But I will amend the definition so far as to say*
*that what all the gods hate is impious, and what they love pious or holy;*
*and what some of them love and others hate is both or neither. Shall this be*
*our definition of piety and impiety?*
*(Again, Socrates tries to pin down the definition of pious, to get a clear*
*concept of it.)*

E: Why not, Socrates?

S: *Why not! Certainly, as far as I am concerned, Euthyphro. But whether*
*this admission will greatly assist you in the task of instructing me as you*
*promised, is a matter for you to consider.*

E: Yes, I should say that what all the gods love is pious and holy, and the
opposite, which they all hate, is impious.

S: *Ought we to inquire into the truth of this, Euthyphro, or simply to accept*
*the mere statement on our own authority and that of others?*

E: We should inquire, and I believe that the statement will stand the test of
inquiry.

S: *That, my good friend, we shall know better in a little while. The point*
*which I should first wish to understand is whether the pious or holy is*
*beloved by the gods because it is holy, or holy because it is beloved of the*
*gods.*
*(Here Socrates makes an important conceptual move. And he circles back*
*on it several times throughout this dialogue, using different analogies, some*
*of which have been excluded from this excerpt. Socrates is arguing that just*
*because the gods believe something to be true does not make it true. Rather,*
*there are some things that are holy and pious irrespective of whether the*
*gods believe that they are. In other words, the gods cannot define what is*
*holy simply by consensus. Even if none of them believed something to be*
*pious and holy, their belief or disbelief would have no bearing on whether*
*something is or is not pious. It is important to note that, in making this*
*argument, Socrates is, in essence, distinguishing between ethics and*
*theology. Interestingly, for the most part, his students, including Plato,*

*failed to make this distinction, instead tending to view ethics and religion as one and the same domain.)*

E: I don't understand your meaning, Socrates.

S: *I will endeavor to explain: we speak of carrying and we speak of being carried, of leading and being led, seeing and being seen. And here is a difference, the nature of which you understand.*

E: I think that I understand.

S: *And is not that which is beloved distinct from that which loves?*

E: Certainly.

S: *Well, and now tell me, is that which is carried in this state of carrying because it is carried, or for some other reason?*

E: No, that is the reason.

S: *And what do you say about piety, Euthyphro? Is not piety, according to your definition, loved by all the gods?*

E: Yes.

S: *Because it is pious or holy, or for some other reason?*

E: No, that is the reason.

S: *It is loved because it is holy, not holy because it is loved.*

E: Yes.

S: *And that which is in a state to be loved of the gods, and is dear to them, is in a state to be loved of them because it is loved of them?*

E: Certainly.

S: *Then that which is loved of God, Euthyphro, is not holy, nor is that which is holy loved of God, as you affirm; but they are two different things.*

E: How do you mean Socrates?

S: *I mean to say that the holy has been acknowledged by us to be loved of God because it is holy, not to be holy because it is loved.*

E: Yes.

S: *But that which is dear to the gods is dear to them because it is loved by them, not loved by them because it is dear to them.*
*(Again, Socrates is making an important conceptual move by saying that just because something is loved by the gods does not mean it is pious—rather, that there must be some distinct essence of pious that holds true, whether or not the gods, or anyone else, believes it to be true.)*

E: True.

S: *But friend Euthyphro, if that which is holy is the same as that which is dear to God, and that which is holy is loved as being holy, then that which is dear to God would have been loved as being dear to God; but if that which is dear to God is dear to him because loved by him, then that which is holy would have been holy because loved by him. But now you see that the reverse is the case, and that they are quite different from one another. For one is of a kind to be loved because it is loved, and the other is loved because it is of a kind to be loved. Thus you appear to me, Euthyphro, when I ask you what is the essence of holiness, to offer an attribute only, and not the essence of holiness, to offer an attribute only, and not the essence—the attribute of being loved by all the gods. But you still refuse to explain to me the nature of piety. And therefore, if you please, I will ask you not to hide your treasure, but to tell me once more what piety or holiness really is, whether dear to the gods or not (for that is a matter about which we will not quarrel). And what is impiety?*

*(The main point that Socrates is making is in this phrase, excerpted from the statement above: "For one is of a kind to be loved because it is loved, and the other is loved because it is of a kind to be loved." Socrates goes to the root of ethics in making this point, and putting his point in the most general of terms—that you can't define ethics by saying that if something is loved by some group of gods or people, then it is good to love that thing. Rather, some things should be loved, in and of themselves, whether they are in fact loved by anyone whatsoever.)*

E: I really do not know, Socrates, how to say what I mean, for somehow or other our arguments, on whatever ground we will rest them, seem to turn round and walk away.

S: *As the notions are your own, you must find some other gibe, for they certainly, as you yourself allow, show an inclination to be on the move.*

E: Nay, Socrates, I shall still say that you are the [one] who sets arguments in motion; not I, certainly, make them move or go around, for they would never have stirred, as far as I am concerned.

*(Euthyphro admits to his intellectual laziness when he says, "they [the ideas] would never have stirred, as far as I am concerned." In other words, he doesn't care to do the kind of deep intellectual work necessary to develop as a thinker. He doesn't care to think deeply about the concepts of pious and impious, and in this statement indirectly insults Socrates as causing arguments to "seem to turn round and walk away." By making this move, he doesn't have to take anything Socrates is saying seriously. He implies that Socrates is overly concerned with ideas or issues that really should be of little or no concern.)*

S: *As I perceive you are indolent, I will myself endeavor to show you how you might instruct me in the nature of piety; and I hope that you will not grudge your labor. Tell me, then, is not that which is pious necessarily just?*

E: Yes.

S: *And is, then, all which is just pious? Or, is that which is pious all just, but that which is just only in part and not all pious?*

E: I don't understand you Socrates.

S: *That was the sort of question which I meant to raise when asking whether the just is the pious, or the pious the just; as whether there may not be justice where there is not always piety; for justice is the more extended notion of which piety is only a part. Do you agree with that?*

*(Socrates gives us a brief answer to the question he has been raising—by stating that everything that is pious is just, but that justice goes beyond what is pious. In other words, what is considered pious is a subset of what is just. He is drawing a conceptual distinction between "just" and "pious".)*

E: Yes, that, I think is correct.

S: *I want you to tell me what part of justice is piety or holiness, that I may be able to tell Meletus not to do me injustice, or indict me for impiety.*

*(Socrates is now trying to nail down precisely what part of justice is pious, since he has been indicted for impiety.)*

E: Piety, or holiness, Socrates, appear to me to be that part of justice which attends to the gods, as there is the other part of justice which attends to men.

S: *What is the meaning of "attention?" For attention can hardly be used in the same sense when applied to the gods as when applied to other things. For instance, horses are said to require attention, and not every person is able to attend to them, but only a person skilled in horsemanship. Is not that true?*

*(Socrates is pointing out the vagueness of Euthyphro's response by saying that giving "attention" can mean different things. He is asking for clarification.)*

E: Quite true.

S: *And is not attention always designed for the good or benefit of that which the attention is given? As in the case of horses, you may observe that when attended to by the horseman's art they are benefited and improved, are they not?*

E: True.

S: *As the dogs are benefited by the huntsmen's art, and the oxen by the art of the oxherd, and all other things are tended or attended for their good and not for their hurt?*

E: Certainly not for their hurt.

S: *But for their good?*

E: Of course.

S: *And does piety or holiness, which has been defined as the art of attending to the gods, benefit or improve them? Would you say that when you do a holy act you make any of the gods better?*

*(Socrates is pointing out that a common meaning of "giving attention" is to improve that which you are attending to, and then asking whether, given Euthyphro's use of this phrase, he is implying that people need to attend to the gods, that people need to improve the gods. Again, this is a basic conceptual move, which illustrates the importance of choosing words carefully.)*

E: No, no; that is certainly not my meaning.

S: *Indeed, Euthyphro, I did not suppose this was your meaning; far otherwise. And that was the reason why I asked you the nature of this attention, because I thought that this was not your meaning...but I must still ask what is this attention to the gods which is called piety?*

E: It is such, Socrates, as servants show to their masters.

S: *I understand—a sort of ministration to the gods.*

E: Exactly.

S: *Tell me—what is that fair work which the gods do by the help of us as their ministers?*

E: Many and fair, Socrates, are the works which they do.

S: *And of the many and fair things which the gods do, which is the chief and principal one?*

E: I have told you already, Socrates. Let me simply say that piety is learning how to please the gods in word and deed, by prayers and sacrifices. That is piety, which is the salvation of families and states, just as the impious, which is unpleasing to the gods, is their ruin and destruction.

S: *I think that you could have answered in much fewer words the chief question which I asked, Euthyphro, if you had chosen. But I see plainly that you are not disposed to instruct me: else why, when we had reached the point, did you turn aside? Had you only answered me I should have learned of you by this time the nature of piety. Now, as the asker of a question is necessarily dependent on the answerer, whither he leads I must follow; and can only ask again, what is the pious, and what is piety? Do you mean that*

*they are a sort of science of praying and sacrificing?*
*(Socrates comes back to his original question, What is piety? Following*
*up Euthyphro's comment, Socrates then attempts to pin down Euthyphro's*
*concept of pious by asking whether it is "a sort of science of praying and*
*sacrificing.")*
E: Yes, I do.

S: *And sacrificing is giving to the gods, and prayer is asking of the gods?*
E: Yes, Socrates.

S: *Upon this view, then, piety, is a science of asking and giving?*
E: You understand me capitally, Socrates.

S: *Yes, my friend; the reason is that I am a votary of your science, and give my*
*mind to it, and therefore nothing which you say will be thrown away upon*
*me. Please then to tell me, what is the nature of this service to the gods? Do*
*you mean that we prefer requests and give gifts to them?*
E: Yes, I do.

S: *Is not the right way of asking to ask of them what we want?*
E: Certainly.

S: *And the right way of giving is to give to them in return what they want of*
*us. There would be no meaning in an art which gives to any one that which*
*he does not want.*
E: Very true, Socrates.

S: *Then piety, Euthyphro, is an art in which gods and men have of doing*
*business with one another?*
E: That is an expression which you may use if you like.

S: *But I have no particular liking for anything but the truth. I wish, however,*
*that you would tell me what benefit accrues to the gods from our gifts. That*
*they are the givers of every good to us is clear; but how we can give any*
*good thing to them in return is far from being equally clear. If they give*
*everything and we give nothing, that must be an affair of business in which*
*we have very greatly the advantage of them.*
*(Socrates is questioning how it would be possible to give gifts to the gods,*
*implying that the very idea is illogical.)*
E: And do you imagine, Socrates, that any benefit accrues to the gods from
what they receive of us?
*(Euthyphro attempts to divert the course of the discussion, to avoid*
*Socrates' question by asking a question of his own, but note how, in the*
*next statement, Socrates repeats his question, attempting to hold Euthyphro*
*responsible for what he says, asking him to support his conclusions with*
*evidence.)*

S: *But if not, Euthyphro, what sort of gifts do we confer upon the gods?*

E: What should we confer upon them, but tributes of honor; and, as I was just now saying, what is pleasing to them?

S: *Piety, then, is pleasing to the gods, but not beneficial or dear to them?*
   *(Socrates is pointing out the illogical inference Euthyphro has made—that something can be pleasing to the gods while not being dear to them. He wants Euthyphro to see the similar meaning of the word "pleasing" and the word "dear.")*

E: I should say that nothing should be dearer.

S: *Then once more the assertion is repeated that piety is dear to the gods?*

E: No doubt.

S: *And when you say this, can you wonder at your words not standing firm, but walking away?…for the argument, as you will perceive, comes round to the same point. I think that you must remember our saying that the holy or pious was not the same as that which is loved of the gods. Do you remember that?*

E: I do.

S: *And do you not see that what is loved of the gods is holy, and that this is the same as what is dear to them?*

E: True.

S: *Then either we were wrong in that admission; or, if we were right then, we are wrong now.*

E: I suppose that is the case.

S: *Then we must begin again and ask, What is piety? That is an inquiry which I shall never be weary of pursuing as far as in me lies; and I entreat you not to scorn me, but to apply your mind to the utmost, and tell me the truth. For, if any man knows, you are he; and therefore I shall detain you until you tell. For if you had not certainly known the nature of piety and impiety, I am confident that you would never, on behalf of a serf, have charged your aged father with murder. You would not have run such a risk of doing wrong in the sight of the gods, and you would have had too much respect for the opinions of men. I am sure, therefore, that you know the nature of piety and impiety. Speak out then, my dear Euthyphro, and do not hide your knowledge.*
   *(Socrates seems to be, for the second time in this dialogue, calling on Euthyphro to persevere through the difficulties in the issue, to think more deeply and with a greater sense of commitment about what he is proclaiming, and to see that what he says is contradictory. One inference we can draw from this dialogue is that Socrates was continually seeking the*

*truth in a discussion. He was good at detecting conceptual inconsistencies [most likely because he routinely practiced thinking critically], and was perplexed at the fact that others did not share his passion for getting at the truth. Through this dialogue, we sense that neither Socrates nor Euthyphro came to closure on the meaning of piety. Nevertheless, through this dialogue, Socrates wants to show Euthyphro either:*

1. *That Euthyphro clearly understands what would please the gods, in which case he would be, from that understanding, able to determine definitively whether he was doing the right thing in charging his father [in other words, doing what would be pleasing to the gods], or*

2. *That Euthyphro is not clear on what would please the gods, and therefore, not justified in pursing action against his father. In this case, Socrates seems to imply that people should not act unless and until they are certain that they are doing what is ethical in the situation.)*

E: Another time, Socrates; for I am in a hurry, and must go now.

S: *Alas! My companion, and will you leave me in despair? I was hoping that you would instruct me in the nature of piety and impiety, so that I might have cleared myself of Meletus and his indictment. Then I might have proved to him that I had been converted by Euthyphro, and had done with rash innovations and speculations, in which I had indulged through ignorance, and was about to lead a better life.*

# Appendix C

## More On Socrates[3]

In this section, we briefly elaborate the contribution of Socrtes to critical thinking. This section should be viewed as a follow-up to the section "On Socrates" in Part Five.

### Socrates' Emphasis on Living an Ethical Life

We understand Socrates to be a person of high intellectual courage and ethical integrity, a person not only committed to living an ethical life, but also committed to helping others do the same. Socrates clearly understood intellectual development and intellectual perseverance as requisite to ethical reasoning. As we can see from the following description, Socrates believed that the reason people behave in unethical ways results from a lack of intellectual skill—that mistakes in reasoning are the root cause of unethical action.

> The intellectual gifts of Socrates were hardly less remarkable than his moral virtues. Naturally observant, acute, and thoughtful, he developed these qualities by constant and systematic use. The exercise of the mental powers was, he conceived, no mere occupation of leisure hours, but rather a sacred and ever-present duty; because, moral error being intellectual error translated into act, he who would live virtuously must first rid himself of ignorance and folly. By the careful study of the ethical problems which met him in himself and others he acquired a remarkable tact in dealing with questions of practical morality; and in the course of the life-long war he waged against vagueness of thought and laxity of speech he made himself a singularly apt and ready reasoner (p. 332).

At the heart of his thinking and his work was a focus on ethical concepts and principles. Above everything else, Socrates wanted people to realize that living an ethical life required developing one's intellectual abilities, that right living was possible only through right thinking. In other words, he wanted people to see that a desire to live ethically is not sufficient to living an ethical life—that good intentions are not enough. Rather, because ethical issues are often complex, developed intellectual skills are necessary for reasoning through ethical issues.

Aware of the importance of ethical concepts to ethical reasoning, Socrates placed the delineation of ethical concepts at the center of his dialectic method. Repeatedly, throughout the Socratic dialogues, we find an emphasis on defining ethical concepts, and then relating those concepts to actual cases and analogies.

Perhaps purposefully, Socrates laid the groundwork for what would later become the *study of ethics*, bringing together and clearly delineating a cluster of ethical concepts and principles upon which the basis for ethical reasoning still largely rests. Through his work, he made clear the important role of intellectual discipline and intellectual autonomy in ethical reasoning. He highlighted the fact that no one could think for another, that each

---

[3] All of the quotes in this appendix come from the following source unless otherwise indicated: *Encyclopedia Britannica*, Eleventh Edition, 1911. All blue text is reference material.

person must develop skills of mind and use those skills in reasoning through life's many complex problems and issues.

## Focusing on Foundational Concepts and Issues

We can see in the Socratic dialogues, that through probing questions Socrates attempted to understand, and help others understand, how to live a rational and just life. He often did this by focusing on a specific ethical concept, attempting to get increasingly closer to the essence of the concept. Consider the following description of his method, written by Xenophon:[4]

> [Socrates] was always conversing about human beings—examining what is pious, what is impious, what is noble, what is shameful, what is just, what is unjust, what is moderation, what is madness, what is courage, what is cowardice, what is a city, what is a statesman, what is rule over human beings, what is a skilled ruler over human beings, as well as the other things, knowledge of which he believed makes one a gentleman (noble and good), while those who are ignorant of them would justly be called slavish (pp. 4–5).

## The Two Primary Processes of the Socratic Method

Let us briefly consider the two primary processes inherent in the Socratic method, the destructive, and the constructive process (as described in the *Encyclopedia Britanica*):

> In the application of the "dialectic" method two process are distinguishable—the destructive process, by which the worse opinion was eradicated, and the constructive process, by which the better opinion was induced.

Though Socrates felt it important for people to reach and work through the constructive process *if possible*, he nevertheless thought that the destructive process was useful in-and-of itself:

> "Before I ever met you," says Meno in a Socratic dialogue by Plato, "I was told that you spent your time in doubting and leading others to doubt: and it is a fact that your witcheries and spells have brought me to that condition; you are like the torpedo: as it benumbs any one who approaches and touches it, so do you. For myself, my soul and my tongue are benumbed, so that I have no answer to give you." Even if, as often happened, the respondent, baffled and disgusted by the destructive process, at this point withdrew from the inquiry, he had, in Socrates' judgment, gained something: for whereas formerly, being ignorant, he had supposed himself to have knowledge, now, being ignorant, he was in some sort conscious of his ignorance, and accordingly would be for the future more circumspect in action (p. 335).

Still, Socrates viewed the constructive process as vitally important to intellectual development:

> Of the two processes of the dialectical method, the destructive process attracted more attention, both in consequence of its novelty and because of those who willingly

---

[4] Xenophon, a student of Socrates, wrote about the life and practices of Socrates shortly after Socrates' indictment and death. This quote is taken from the following source: *Xenophon: Memorabilia*. 1994. Ithaca, NY: Cornell University Press.

or unwillingly submitted to it stopped short at the stage of "perplexity." But to Socrates and his intimates the constructive process was the proper and necessary sequel (p. 336).

## Uncovering Unconscious Thoughts

An important part of the destructive process in the Socratic method was uncovering irrational thoughts. Socrates recognized the self-deceptive tendencies of the human mind, and thought that the reason people behaved irrationally or unethically was due to the fact that they were using faulty reasoning, reasoning that seemed logical on the surface, but was actually flawed. He recognized, therefore, that one must bring unconscious thoughts to the level of conscious awareness in order to examine them. This point is elaborated in the *Encyclopedia Britanica:*

> In general, it was not mere "ignorance" with which Socrates had to contend, but "ignorance mistaking itself for knowledge" or "false conceit of wisdom." —a more stubborn and formidable foe, who, safe so long as he remained in his entrenchments, must be drawn from them, circumvented, and surprised. Accordingly, taking his departure from some apparently remote principle or proposition to which the respondent yielded a ready assent, Socrates would draw from it an unexpected but undeniable consequence which was plainly inconsistent with the opinion impugned. In this way, he brought his interlocutor to pass judgment upon himself, and reduced him to a state of "doubt" or "perplexity" (p. 335).

## Formulating General Principles By Which to Live

Now consider the constructive process. What we see in the following passage is a deliberate focus on helping the answerer formulate a general principle, through uses of analogy, that could be applied to future situations.

> If, however, having been thus convinced of ignorance, the respondent did not shrink from a new effort, Socrates was ready to aid him by further questions of a suggestive sort. Consistent thinking with a view to consistent action being the end of the inquiry, Socrates would direct the respondent's attention to instances analogous to that in hand, and so lead him to frame for himself a generalization from which the passions and the prejudices of the moment were, as far as might be, excluded. In this constructive process, though the element of surprise was no longer necessary, the interrogative form was studiously preserved, because it secured, at each step, the conscious and responsible assent of the learner (pp. 335–336).

Note the following explication of the system inherent in Socratic dialogues:

> What, then, were the positive conclusions to which Socrates carried his hearers? And how were those positive conclusions obtained? Turning to Xenophon for an answer, we note (1) that the recorded conversations are concerned with practical action, political, moral, or artistic; (2) that in general there is a process from the known to the unknown through a generalization, expressed or implied; (3) that the generalizations are sometimes rules of conduct, justified by examination of known instances, sometimes definitions similarly established (p. 336).

## The Influence of Socrates

Socrates' views are unique in the history of ideas. However, the implications of his approach as a practical means of pursuing personal and intellectual integrity have never been fully realized. With the rebirth of interest in the practical application of critical thinking to everyday learning, however, the Socratic art is being given a new hearing. Perhaps one day it will be an intrinsic part of teaching at all levels.

# The Thinker's Guide Library

The Thinker's Guide series provides convenient, inexpensive, portable references that students and faculty can use to improve the quality of studying, learning, and teaching. Their modest cost enables instructors to require them of all students (in addition to a textbook). Their compactness enables students to keep them at hand whenever they are working in or out of class. Their succinctness serves as a continual reminder of the most basic principles of critical thinking.

## For Students & Faculty

**Critical Thinking**—The essence of critical thinking concepts and tools distilled into a 19-page pocket-size guide. (1–24 copies $4.00 each; 25–199 copies $2.00 each; 200–499 copies $1.75 each) #520m

**Analytic Thinking**—This guide focuses on the intellectual skills that enable one to analyze anything one might think about — questions, problems, disciplines, subjects, etc. It provides the common denominator between all forms of analysis. (1–24 copies $6.00 each; 25–199 copies $4.00 each; 200–499 copies $2.50 each) #595m

**Asking Essential Questions**—Introduces the art of asking essential questions. It is best used in conjunction with the Miniature Guide to Critical Thinking and the How to Study mini-guide. (1–24 copies $6.00 each; 25–199 copies $4.00 each; 200–499 copies $2.50 each) #580m

**How to Study & Learn**—A variety of strategies—both simple and complex—for becoming not just a better student, but also a master student. (1–24 copies $6.00 each; 25–199 copies $4.00 each; 200–499 copies $2.50 each) #530m

**How to Read a Paragraph**—This guide provides theory and activities necessary for deep comprehension. Imminently practical for students. (1–24 copies $6.00 each; 25–199 copies $4.00 each; 200–499 copies $2.50 each) #525m

**How to Write a Paragraph**—Focuses on the art of substantive writing. How to say something worth saying about something worth saying something about. (1–24 copies $6.00 each; 25–199 copies $4.00 each; 200–499 copies $2.50 each) #535m

**The Human Mind**—Designed to give the reader insight into the basic functions of the human mind and to how knowledge of these functions (and their interrelations) can enable one to use one's intellect and emotions more effectively. (1–24 copies $5.00 each; 25–199 copies $2.50 each; 200–499 copies $1.75 each) #570m

**Foundations of Ethical Reasoning**—Provides insights into the nature of ethical reasoning, why it is so often flawed, and how to avoid those flaws. It lays out the function of ethics, its main impediments, and its social counterfeits. (1–24 copies $6.00 each; 25–199 copies $4.00 each; 200–499 copies $2.50 each) #585m

**How to Detect Media Bias and Propaganda**—Designed to help readers come to recognize bias in their nation's news and to recognize propaganda so that they can reasonably determine what media messages need to be supplemented, counter-balanced or thrown out entirely. It focuses on the internal logic of the news as well as societal influences on the media. (1–24 copies $6.00 each; 25–199 copies $4.00 each; 200–499 copies $2.50 each) #575m

**Scientific Thinking**—The essence of scientific thinking concepts and tools. It focuses on the intellectual skills inherent in the well-cultivated scientific thinker. (1–24 copies $6.00 each; 25–199 copies $4.00 each; 200–499 copies $2.50 each) #590m

**Fallacies: The Art of Mental Trickery and Manipulation**—Introduces the concept of fallacies and details 44 foul ways to win an argument. (1–24 copies $6.00 each; 25–199 copies $4.00 each; 200–499 copies $2.50 each) #533m

**Critical Thinking for Children**—Designed for K–6 classroom use. Focuses on explaining basic critical thinking principles to young children using cartoon characters. (1–24 copies $5.00 each; 25–199 copies $2.50 each; 200–499 copies $1.75 each) #540m

# For Faculty

**Active and Cooperative Learning**—Provides 27 simple ideas for the improvement of instruction. It lays the foundation for the ideas found in the mini-guide How to Improve Student Learning. (1–24 copies $3.00 each; 25–199 copies $1.50 each; 200–499 copies $1.25 each) #550m

**How to Improve Student Learning**—Provides 30 practical ideas for the improvement of instruction based on critical thinking concepts and tools. It cultivates student learning encouraged in the How to Study and Learn mini-guide. (1–24 copies $6.00 each; 25–199 copies $4.00 each; 200–499 copies $2.50 each) #560m

**Critical and Creative Thinking**—Focuses on the interrelationship between critical and creative thinking through the essential role of both in learning. (1–24 copies $6.00 each; 25–199 copies $4.00 each; 200–499 copies $2.50 each) #565m

**Critical Thinking Reading and Writing Test**—Assesses the ability of students to use reading and writing as tools for acquiring knowledge. Provides grading rubrics and outlines five levels of close reading and substantive writing. (1–24 copies $6.00 each; 25–199 copies $4.00 each; 200–499 copies $2.50 each) #563m

**Socratic Questioning**—Focuses on the mechanics of Socratic dialogue, on the conceptual tools that critical thinking brings to Socratic dialogue, and on the importance of questioning in cultivating the disciplined mind. (1–24 copies $6.00 each; 25–199 copies $4.00 each; 200–499 copies $2.50 each) #553m

**Critical Thinking Competency Standards**— Provides a framework for assessing students' critical thinking abilities. (1–24 copies $6.00 each; 25–199 copies $4.00 each; 200–499 copies $2.50 each) #555m